"Just Because My Husband's A Woman..."

Marcy's side of the story

Marcy M. Madden

DEDICATION

To My Beloved Scottie-who has my heart and my deepest gratitude for teaching me what true love is, for being my inspiration in all things, and for agreeing to my request to allow me "to be new."

Zuzubean Press
www.zuzubean.com

Contact the author for questions, booking and appearance
schedule at marcy@zuzubean.com

ACKNOWLEDGEMENTS

My deepest gratitude to dear friends and family and acquaintances who heard what Scottie and I were going through, found out we were staying in our marriage, and told me I should write a book. To those special beings I talk about in this book who uplifted and held me, encouraged me, were cheerleaders for my strengths, and angels when I wasn't strong, and who could make me laugh when I most needed to. To the spiritual warriors who tread the path with me, you know who you are! To Jacob who has always been a shining light since the day we met. You have given me more than can ever be measured. To Jo who read my first draft and offered great input and encouragement, and who introduced me to my favorite actress, Judith Light, who hugged me and told me how glad she is that I'm sharing my story. To Elana for her generous and insightful suggestions, who made this book better and taught me a lot about writing. To Tia for her valuable comments and encouragement. To Catherine and Mark whose generous endorsements brought tears to my eyes and boosted my confidence that I do have something to say. To my dedicated Editor, Clare Newbury, whose support, and humor, and virtual red pencil were a boon to me, and to every page. I have a new friend. To Adam, whose design brought this book to life, and whose friendship is unparalleled. To MyLove, partner in life, in love, in spirit, in work, in publishing, and in all things, who has held my hand throughout our life together.

Thank you!

TABLE OF CONTENTS

FOREWORD OR SOMETHING?

"You should write a book," people say. Well, my spouse wrote one (we're still working on that word. Not "book," "spouse." What do I call ... Scottie?).

For over 20 years, we were together as husband and wife. We celebrated our 28th wedding anniversary on April 29, 2017.

But the thing is, Scottie is not my husband. I guess.

Perhaps you've surmised by now, Scottie is a woman; not the man I thought I fell in love with and married those many years ago. She wrote a book about her life's journey—flashing back on childhood experiences, talking about the pain of having to conceal who she really was and, finally, her coming out. Her book is called, "Getting Back To Me" from girl to boy to woman in just 50 years.

Honestly, this revelation devastated me when she came out to me. Any carpet I had stood on was pulled right out from under me. I was lost. I felt alone; abandoned. Something inside me died. Or so it felt at the time.

So, maybe it is time for me to tell my story—offer my side of the equation. I'm sure I'm not the first spouse of a transgender person to write a book. But I think I have insights, experiences, lessons to offer, because I had quite the arc to traverse, to where I ended up. Never fear; the light at the end of the tunnel is not a train.

Here's just one example of where my journey began regarding the subject of transgender. I was watching an Oprah show one day. Oprah interviewed a couple where the husband had transitioned and was living as the woman she always felt herself to be. They had kids and they were staying together. They said they were happy and that keeping the family together was of greatest importance. I just didn't get it. I literally looked at the TV and said out loud, "Well! At least I'll never have to deal with that!" Oh, really?!

I never would have guessed that that would be exactly what I would have to deal with.

So, I will be honest with you about it all; about me. Who I was, what it took, and who I became.

If this book offers any reassurance, inspiration, or helps expand someone's understanding of what it is to be transgender and to be their spouse, I will have accomplished my goal.

At least you can learn the importance of never saying "never!"

Oh! And having a sense of humor also helps.

CHAPTER 1
SNAPSHOT

I am not new to the marriage game. For a while, I started to believe that I got married a few times just because I liked a party thrown in my honor! That's not really true. I was looking for love (OK, you can finish the lyric, if you know it!). But where did that searching come from? Why was finding love so important to me? I think it started very early from experiences in my childhood. Here's a snapshot of my early years.

I grew up in a storybook setting in the '50s. We lived in a large, Century-old colonial house on a hill in Fitchburg, Massachusetts. We had 3.5 acres of land surrounded by woods and other large homes which were occupied with friends to match all the generations in our family. We were safe and free to be out all day until dusk during the summer. We could take off on endless bike rides or swim in a neighbor's pool. I can completely call on all my senses to take me back there again.

My friend, Barbie, lived just up the hill. I could cut through her grandparents' property, past that swimming pool where the whole neighborhood was welcome, and then cross the country street to Barbie's house. We'd play for hours, acting out scenes from our girlhood fantasies with her giant doll house, or in the woods behind their home where we would kiss trees pretending they were our boyfriends. Troy Donahue for Barb, Tab Hunter or Richard Chamberlain for me. A punchline on that comes later.

I can hear Mrs. Kemp's voice as clear as it was then when she would call to us and say, "Barb, Dear, it's time for Marce to run along home."

When we weren't playing house or off on a bike adventure, Barbie, and our assorted siblings and neighbors, would be at the pool for hours on end during the summer. Another regular was our splash-happy Welsh Terrier, Rusty, who had to join in every game we played.

We'd be in the water until our parents called us out because we were shivering and our lips were blue. Barbie and I would lie side-by-side on our towels that we'd spread out on the grass. The sun was warm, and we'd drink it in because we were shivering so hard. Then there was that feeling of just starting to warm up, the shivers getting more intermittent, right when a cloud would pass over. Torture! I'd watch the cloud as it took its time to drift across the sun and steal my warmth. Any time now that I can go outside, lie on my back and look at the sky, I am instantly transported to those sweet, long days of summer when life was so carefree. I smell the grass and the subtle scent of chlorine from the pool mixed with the cigarette smoke of the adults. I hated that they smoked, but there was something about that mixture of odors that was pleasing to me then.

My parents had a very loving relationship. They looked happy, talked to each other all the time, and my father always gave my mother a movie dip kiss when he came home from work at the end of the day. Then they would sit and have cocktails while he downloaded his various work challenges. He wasn't just venting, he was looking for her wisdom to help him with whatever the situation was. And she did. She was bright and an accomplished student of human nature.

So, with my parents' obvious love and my Richard Chamberlain tree kisses, I did have a storybook picture of what my Prince Charming would be like, and how we would be so in love, so loving, forever.

Lest my description of my early years in Fitchburg sounds too idyllic, it wasn't always peace and love. And, as I look back on that time, I have become more clear about how many conflicting, or at least confusing, messages I got.

In fact, delving into what went into making me *me* for this memoir has brought up some memories I'd completely forgotten, and that turns out to be quite poignant. I'll point them out as we go along, but the end result is that I can see the patterns that kept recurring in my life better—the weaving of events and my experiences of them, and how that shaped my understanding of life, love and relationships.

I was the third kid of four in my family. Brother one, then two years later, brother two, then four years later, me, then four years later, brother three.

When people would ask my mother how many kids she had, she'd say, "I have four boys and one's a girl." Conflicting message number one!

In light of where this story is going, I think we can all agree that little tidbit is somewhat ironic. Right?

From the time I was one year old, my grandparents lived with us until their deaths. My grandfather had been a very successful businessman in Cleveland, Ohio, and even played baseball in the minor leagues. It was a blow to him as well as my grandmother and my mother when he lost everything in the stock market crash. My dad, generous beyond belief, took in his in-laws to live with us just about the time I was born.

We called my grandfather "Doden." I think that we had adopted the name my mother had always called him. He was not well by the time he was living with us, so he wasn't very visible. He kept to his room and was off limits to us for the most part. If baseball was on TV, that's where he was.

I just have two memories of Doden that stand out to me. One is of the day he fixed my roller skates. I had the old-fashioned kind that had a special key to unlock the frame so they could be shortened or lengthened depending on your shoe size. They then attached to the bottom of your shoes. Even though he was in the middle of watching a baseball game on TV, Doden turned to me when I came into his room with my skates and took to adjusting them so they would fit on my shoes and I could go skating. That time stands out to me, I guess because it was one of the few instances when he paid attention to me. He was focused on helping me out, and I loved that expression of caring. In fact, I remember his smile when he handed me back my skates. It has stayed with me since.

The other memory is of one of our family dinners: We always gathered in the dining room for a formal dinner at night. My dad would put on a sport coat for the occasion and my mother would have cooked a full, delicious meal, healthy by the standards of the day. I would set the table with placemats, candles, silverware and napkins. We would have some form of meat—steak, roast, leg of lamb—that my dad would carve at the sideboard. He would hand me plates after serving the meat, and I would take them to the assigned places at the table. Vegetables and potatoes or salad would be in silver dishes on the table where we would serve ourselves and then pass them on. When we were all home, there would be eight of us at the table for a sit-down dinner—my parents, we four children and my two grandparents. We would often spend hours there in the candlelight talking about our day or playing some form of word game.

There were also ample table manner lessons! Though that felt tedious and overbearing at the time, I've since become grateful for knowing to sit up straight, what forks to use for what, how to serve from the left; take from the right, etc. It means I can go anywhere and be appropriate, even at the most formal of dinner occasions.

But it's not as if these nights were stiff and somber! We laughed and joked and punned all through the meal. And the household was relaxed enough that our parakeet, Friday, was free to fly around wherever he pleased. One night, he joined us in the dining room during dinner. He stomped around on the table surface, sometimes land on the nose of dad's (bird!) hunting dog who was trying to remember that this bird was different and he must not touch it. After a couple such excursions, Friday proceeded to fly back to the table and land squarely in the mashed potatoes on my grandfather's plate. That was cause enough for us to giggle, but when he proceeded to fly up onto Doden's mostly bald head, we lost it! He walked around leaving dollops of potato all across Doden's scalp, some of it getting tangled in what hair he had left. Doden was equally amused at the bird's antics, but then my mother signaled to my brother, Morgan, to remove the bird and put him in his cage for the rest of our meal.

I love remembering those events fondly because, as I said, Doden was away in his room most of the time and I didn't see him much.

On the other hand, my grandmother was very visible and involved in our everyday life. Our nickname for her was "Ava," don't ask me why. She helped out with the housework wherever she could, and she also became our self-appointed babysitter/nanny whenever my parents weren't home. And she was very . . . strict! She definitely believed in dishing out punishment when we disobeyed her or did something wrong in her book. Spilling and breaking things was at least a misdemeanor.

Then there were capitol offenses. For example, some of those long bike rides I took royally pissed off my grandmother. She did not appreciate that I was gone so long without anyone knowing where I was. Time for a lesson!

We had a large forsythia bush out at the end of the driveway. Beautiful, delicate, yellow blossoms, and the best, flexible branches for making switches to whip our legs with. How stupid was I that I obeyed my grandmother when she sent me out to cut a switch—for me! I'd bring back a branch and watch her break off the flowers, and then came the stinging pain on my calves and the sharp words in her piercing voice.

Of course, this is regarded as abuse now. Luckily (smartly?), I didn't succumb to the switch much; I was a good girl! It was my brothers who drew the fire. I learned the power of honesty. I don't think they have yet!

You may ask if my parents knew about these disciplinary actions. I'm sure this would horrify them. They never laid a hand on us. But I think we kids were afraid enough of my grandmother that we didn't tell on her.

My mother told stories about how she had grown up with Ava's abusiveness herself. She was a wild, independent spirit that could not be tamed by harsh words or being yanked around by her hair. I know that she was determined not to pass on the abuse to us. If she was angry with me, she would say, "I'm really angry right now, so I need some time to cool down, and you can go to your room. We'll talk later about what to do about this." When she would call up to me that I was free to come out of my room, she'd most often say, "I'm sure you've punished yourself enough by now. There's nothing more we need to do. You learned your lesson." And I had! There was nothing worse than thinking I'd displeased my mother. I adored her.

My mother and grandmother had formed a sort of truce under our roof that lasted until my grandmother passed, but they never really achieved peace.

When my grandfather died several years after they moved in with us, Mummy was devastated. Doden had been her rock. He had been her savior and hero when she was young. Always explaining to her how to handle her mother and not cross her. I have a stack of letters he wrote my mother when she was away at school. He was so dear to her. They seem quite formal by today's standards, but you could tell he loved her and wanted the best for her, and was trying to guide her to being a responsible adult. I also have one letter from my grandmother to my mother back then where she's scolding her for being frivolous by asking for some money because her allowance wasn't enough. I'm sure my mother felt she could do nothing right in Ava's eyes, and could do no wrong in Doden's.

She never really got over the loss of her father, and watching his health go downhill in our house was devastating to her. He had taught her so much about life, including how *not* to throw a ball or drive a car like a girl! She used to say, "I was my father's only son." My confusion messages numbers two and three? There will be more of these, but I'm quite sure I'll lose count.

My memories of my grandmother were not all negative

by any means. I loved her very much. The disciplines were few and far between, and she was good to me otherwise. She filled in on a lot of the duties one might expect of a mother.

My mother didn't play with me. I was pretty free to play on my own. I did go on shopping excursions with her, which I loved, whether it was shopping at the A&P, the bookstore, an antique shop … she always took me along. In a way, she treated me like an adult. She wasn't the baby talk type, and rarely, if ever, helped me with my homework. There were some special things she did for me, like making my outfit for my ballet recital or creating amazing Halloween costumes. She was there for me, but more on her own terms. I fit into her world; she didn't join me in mine. So Ava filled in with some of those other activities. She'd be the one to get me up and dressed in the morning, she'd make my breakfast and send me off to school. She helped me with homework, and taught me to sew and bake cakes and pies. I'd help mix the batter and was given the high honor of licking the bowl. We enjoyed our time together. I could feel her love, though she was not at all physically demonstrative. She may not have hugged me, but she did other things to show me that I was special to her. Frankly, I think I was her second chance at having a good relationship with her daughter.

She would often make us a picnic and we'd go for a walk in the woods that stretched for miles behind our house. We went quite a distance before stopping at our favorite stream to sit on our same rock right in the middle of the stream where we would have our sandwiches and dangle our feet in the cool, bubbling water. Sweet summer days out in nature with her.

Honestly, I had forgotten about all this until I went back in time to write in this book about my family and growing up in Fitchburg. I teared up when I recalled these days with Ava and am grateful to visit them again in detail. I teared up because I was transported into those magical moments with her when we were close and we could talk about life. She would tell me about her past, so I got to know more about the whole of who she was as a young woman, and what her life was like as a school teacher, a wife and mother, mistress of their house in town and at their horse farm in the country. I don't think she shared her stories or philosophies with anyone else, and it made me feel special.

It felt like we were two girls on an adventure together on the one hand, and that she was sharing her wisdom with me on the other. It was a side of her I rarely saw when we were at home, and I loved this side of her. She seemed so young and carefree.

Sometimes, we would venture into the woods together to go puff-ball hunting. We'd look for the fungi that grew on the side of birch trees so we could collect them and she would bring them home to cook like a mushroom. Actually pretty tasty. She had such knowledge of nature craft that I sometimes thought she might be a witch. She'd always have a pot of some concoction of bones and herbs and vegetables gurgling away on the back burner. She'd pick wild dandelions in our yard and make sweet and sour dandelion greens as a side dish, which I grew to love. I never could get into the pickled honeycomb tripe, however! Gag me!

Ava was always active—keeping busy with household chores. It was in a room downstairs—the TV/ironing room—that we spent lots of time together. She helped me with my school papers or we'd watch Perry Mason together.

I especially remember one cold, wintry New England

New Year's Eve when she let me stay up to watch the ball come down in Times Square. That was a milestone. I was growing up. We toasted in the new year together.

A few years later, on another one of those cold, dark evenings, we sat together on the old chaise in her room talking, and she was working on one of her signature hook rugs. Something moved me to ask, "Why do you do so much work around the house? Are you trying to pay Daddy back for taking care of you?"

She said, "Yes."

It surprised me that she would be so frank. It was also quite touching. This woman had incredible wealth at one time in her life, and now she was more like a live-in maid and nanny. I was moved that she would share something so delicate with me; something so personal. It affirmed our closeness.

That ended up being the night she died.

I was the one who found Ava dead in her room. I was 13. She had had a heart attack days before and was told to rest. That was not easy for her.

I remember the night vividly still. I had brought her dinner to her because she was not supposed to go up and down the stairs.

I went into my parents' room to do homework over the phone with my friend, Christie. Pretty much a nightly event. For you younger readers, phones were hard-wired to the wall in those days. In fact, this was long ago enough that the only phone choice was a black phone with a rotary dial. The cords weren't even spiraled at this point in time. Phone numbers were seven digits long, and started with a word. Our number was "Diamond 3-6831." If you lived in the Diamond zone, you just dialed the 3-6831. Otherwise, it would be Di3-6831.

I think Christie and I were responsible for the birth of

speaker phones. As I sat on my mother's bed, I'd prop the receiver on a pillow so my hands would be free to take notes as Christie and I talked through our assignments, or practiced reciting things we had to memorize.

After our homework session that night, I hung up the phone and prepared what I would say as I walked back to Ava's room. I put a smile on my face and, as I walked through her door, I said, "Do you want some more . . ." but she wasn't there. A strange feeling came over me as I rounded the corner to where I could see the chaise. I didn't see her at first, but then, there she was, lying on the floor in front of it. So small, so quiet, with her hooked rug at her side, like it was auditioning to be her shroud.

I had a premonition when I walked back in her room that night; I just had the feeling this might be the night she would go. I don't know why. In a way, I think it was because she had made her confession to me about her guilt about living off my father.

I had a wave of emotions wash over me when I saw her on the floor, and I couldn't really sort them out. It wasn't as if this was my first experience of death. There were myriad pets who had passed and an assortment of bunnies and birds my cat brought home that I tried, usually unsuccessfully, to save. And there was my grandfather who died in the house and I saw him carried away.

But this was the first time I was alone with a person who died, and she and I had just been talking about a half-hour before. This may sound strange, but there was something eerily perfect about my being the one to find her. Why? I don't know. Because she had been the one to care for me for all those years and now our roles were reversed? I needed to take care of her in her final hours? That might have been part of it. Whatever the reason, it felt like a very private and personal moment between us, and I could bid her farewell alone. It was just the two of us, like all the little secrets we had shared on that rock in the stream years before.

The initial wave of feelings I had when I saw her melted into a surprisingly calm state as I walked past her to go downstairs to tell my parents. This was up to me; I had a message to deliver.

Dad was doing the dishes. My mother was asleep on the couch in the TV room. This had become a more and more common occurrence as she succumbed to her drinking.

So, with her crashed on the couch, I went to Dad first. He would know how to handle this.

"Daddy, please come upstairs. I think Ava died."

I was hoping he'd come up with me just to check, and then we'd figure out what to say to Mummy. But as he started to follow me, he said, "Go get your mother."

I did, and, once she had shaken off the fog of sleep, we all went upstairs where Ava was lying on the floor.

My father checked to see if she was breathing, and covered her body. Then he, my mother, and I sat on Ava's bed to await the ambulance. We didn't talk much. We reminisced about Ava some. I felt deep in my heart that this is when my mother finally made peace with her mother.

I also had a sense of peace—it was the source of that calm I tapped into that night, and it is a part of me that I have to know intimately as my life has unfolded.

CHAPTER 2
GRIMM IS RIGHT!

Did the punishment from my grandmother affect me long-term? I guess conventional wisdom would say "yes." However, though I will focus on many of the less fun moments in my life in this book, I do feel I had a good childhood overall. The good far outweighed the bad in my early life.

I want to look at how my beliefs and experiences influenced my way of thinking and responding to the world around me.

My parents seemed to be so in love and happy. That's what I wanted. I don't think I ever heard them raise their voices to each other or ever saw them fight. Well, that's not quite true. My dad would get upset with my mother once her alcoholism was showing, but I was in my teens then.

I think it's unfortunate that I didn't see my parents fight because maybe that's why my three brothers and I didn't learn how. And forget learning how to fight fair! Oh we fought among ourselves, as siblings will, but there was nothing fair about it. I think the first words I ever heard from my brothers were, "Shut up or I'll pound you," or

"You're cruising for a bruising!" Sweet. "Sucking for a contusion" was my favorite.

Not knowing what a healthy argument or disagreement looked like did influence my skewed perspective on life; not knowing how to adeptly handle disagreement, I dreaded and avoided it.

And then there were the lessons on love itself.

I look back at all those Fairy Tales my parents and Ava read to me—Cinderella, Beauty and the Beast, Sleeping Beauty . . . all beauties, by the way. What's the message for girls there?! And why didn't anyone ever cry foul when those stories of the beauties finding their princes ended at "happily ever after?!" *Really?* That was just the beginning, dummy! We need to know what "happily ever after is!" and what really does happen after. That's where we truly need the coaching and guidance. Jeez!

My parents' relationship and those fairy tales had me convinced that everything should always be rosy. A couple in love would never fight. And, if there was a fight, it must mean something was wrong. Really wrong, deep down inside the relationship.

So, when I was old enough to start entering into relationships, when those times of discord came in any of my relationships, as they inevitably did, I thought the love was gone. That was it. We were through. I would start to pull away; even end up leaving. I figured they were done with me, too, since there was no proclaiming of their undying devotion or begging me to stay.

Anyway, after a string of boyfriends, I ended up with three marriages and three divorces. Each one had its own particular share of lessons. Each one shed just a bit more light on my understanding of what love truly is. Here's a closer look.

CHAPTER 3
THE MARCH OF THE HUSBANDS

My first marriage was when I was 24.

I was living in Marin County, California by this time. It was 1969 and I was back in the states after a year abroad in Geneva, Switzerland. I only meant to visit California, to check out the West Coast before settling in Vermont, which had been my plan. Plans change.

My parents and "baby brother," Doug, had moved to California the year before.

My parents lived in San Francisco when Dad was in the Navy during the war, and he hoped that coming back to the Bay Area would be a fresh start for them. My oldest brother, Macky, had been just a toddler then, and Mum and Dad were quite happy in those early years of their marriage. So, in 1968, when Dad got a great job offer in the city as President of a Paper Company, he jumped at the chance for a change of venue.

My mother's alcoholism had become a real issue by this point and my dad was trying everything he could to help her get past it.

I have spent hours mulling over how this strong, vivacious, popular woman would fall prey to alcohol. Was it partly because she did not want to grow old and have her looks fade—her face get wrinkles and her shape lose its curves? She had been so attractive and popular, I think aging was very hard for her. Sometimes I think it also had to do with her intense effort to avoid the legacy of abuse that she suffered at the hand of her mother. She was determined to raise us with kindness and fairness; not punishment, and I think her effort to keep her temper under lock and key took its toll on her health.

That was a time when alcoholism was treated as a mental illness rather than a physical addiction. But in the years leading up to this, it wasn't seen (or talked about) as that big a problem.

In my mother's case, it felt like her condition had crept up on her. We didn't think this was something that would go on indefinitely. We were in denial. Of course she would get better when she was past menopause or whatever other "reason" she or we were able to give at the time.

I think it's important to point out that this began in the '50s—the cocktail years. Everything revolved around the pre-dinner cocktail(s), having someone "over for drinks," going to cocktail parties or "just one" nightcap. Of course alcoholism was known about back then, but it was not the first assumption one would make when they saw someone tipsy. People just drank a lot then, and going over one's limit was often excused. I know my parents both drank their fair share, but I don't recall seeing them drunk. It seemed they were pretty good at "holding their liquor." See, a whole language formed around this time. Everyone smoked and drank; it's just what they did. It turned out many people were alcoholics, but there was a social stigma about it then, and usually an unspoken agreement to keep it quiet. Unfortunately, my mother was one of those people. She went from social drinker to alcoholic by the mid '60s.

Mummy went through various treatments, including being committed to a mental hospital. That was a losing proposition. True to form, she charmed the doctors into believing she didn't have a problem, and they released her early.

If only we knew then what we know now.

This brings us to the topic of marriage.

By 1972, cancer and alcoholism had taken down this remarkably strong woman.

My mother was dying.

Knowing she didn't have much time left, I thought one gift I could give her before she passed was to see her daughter get married.

Enter Bob, the Investigator for the Marin County Public Defender's Office.

Bob was gorgeous, smart, funny, warm, fit. He had a boat he was restoring which he wanted for waterskiing. He loved working with his hands and had great handyman skills.

I met him through work. I was the receptionist/secretary/bookkeeper in the office of two psychiatrists. He was an investigator for the Public Defender's office, and came to serve a subpoena to one of the doctors who was to determine the mental competence of a murder suspect to stand trial. Strangely, that murderer was already on death row for murder and, this time, had killed another inmate. Yeah, pretty crazy.

But back to Bob. Did I say gorgeous? Bright blue eyes (Paul Newman or Robert Redford blue) and a face that reminded me of Richard Chamberlain when he starred in *Dr. Kildare*. Wow!

He seemed so perfect, I was pinching myself when he showed interest in me.

I helped him work on the boat and on his mother's apartment building in the San Francisco Marina which she promised would be his someday.

Bob was attentive and loving and fun. We had great weekend waterski trips and, before long, I moved in with him.

It was 1969, and unfortunately the fresh start for my parents was short-lived. Within a year after moving to California, Mummy got breast cancer and ended up having a radical mastectomy. She was amazing at how she kept a stiff upper lip for the outside world, but I think it was partly the booze that was numbing her and helping her to look like she was coping. I admit, it was quite a shock when she showed me her chest and there was just one breast and a long, uneven row of scar tissue on the other side. I think she was open to talking about it and showing me the results of her surgery as a way of saying, "See, I can handle this; no big deal." But those breasts had fed her four children and stood her in good stead for all these years. She was always proud of the fact that she breastfed us all and asserted that it was why we had good teeth and a strong immune system. This all just added to the fact that she was aging, had relocated to a place where she had few friends and was home alone a lot.

My mother's health continued to go downhill and she never really bounced back. I think she gave up the will to live. To put it in her words, "enough is too much." There was no way to predict how long she had, but we all knew her time was coming.

So, when Bob proposed, I was elated—not just for my sake, but also for my mother's. As I said, I thought she would rest easy, knowing her daughter had found a husband. We were married in January of 1972 and she died the following December.

Marriage in the early 70s, wow! Rough waters to navigate. I didn't know how to move between the '50's image of a housewife and the footloose, almost hippie-ish life I'd led in the years before.

I felt like I was playing house. We started a big garden, I refinished furniture, painted rooms in our house … did some impressive cooking and baking. But I felt anything but fulfilled.

Not long after we were married, Bob started acting as if he was now done with wooing a woman to be his wife, and could get on about his business. He spent hours in the garden, and would dress in scuzzy clothes and not shave on the weekends. He was not enthusiastic about going to visit my family when I wanted to. I missed them.

I hoped and mulled and wished, but this wasn't "it." Marriage didn't suddenly make me happy and fulfilled and complete. My dreams were not answered by this man, as handsome and good a man as he was. Bob seemed content. It was me, and I didn't know how to talk about what I was feeling. It was a foggy cloud that lay over me, and I couldn't articulate it, even to myself. I do know I wished Bob was more romantic—like he had been when we were dating. We settled into a routine and I didn't feel like his number one focus anymore. The spark was gone and I wasn't sure what to do about it.

Looking back, I can see how naïve and immature I was. It harkens back to my girlhood dreams about falling in love—that you would be in love and live happily ever after. Love should always just be there! I guess I knew how to fall in love, but I knew nothing about sustaining or feeding it. I hated it when people would say "Marriage is work," or that love does fade when you're married. The excitement diminishes, but it is replaced by another kind of love. No! I wanted the excitement to stay always.

Because my mother died eleven months after I was married, she wasn't there for me when I could have benefitted from motherly advice. The only sex advice she'd ever given me was, "The best part is when it's done and you're cuddling." Helpful, wouldn't you say?

So there we were, after several years of marriage, I was getting restless, and Bob seemed distant. Our fun weekends of camping and waterskiing were traded in for buying a house and being responsible adults.

My old programming emerged—if the romance was gone, the marriage must be in trouble.

Enter flirtation with Roger, someone I worked with. I had been working for a few different groups of psychiatrists for my first few years in Marin. I wanted out of that world and volunteered for a non-profit company that produced public service announcements. I started learning about audio production. Roger was one of the two partners in the non-profit. He and his partner also had plans to open a commercial recording studio, which they did succeed in doing. Roger was so witty and funny, much in the style of my punning family. He was interested, attentive and passionate. I saw in him what I thought was missing in my husband. Don't say it. I know.

Now I thought *this* was the "it." So, we got involved. He was married, too. When it seemed we should be together, we both told our spouses and planned to move in together.

I can still feel the pain of telling my husband. Bob did not see this coming at all and asked that we try to save the marriage. Sometimes I think I should have said "yes," but my guilt for having an affair was so strong, it steered me through the next steps. I felt "too far along" with the other guy to turn back. It makes me sad to this day to remember Bob's face on the awful day I met him at his work to get the signed divorce papers. I stood in the elevator as the doors closed on that gorgeous man who stood looking at me with sadness in his eyes. My eyes are tearing up right now thinking of it.

I had regrets for what I'd done. I even told Roger that I thought we should see other people and not live together right away. He was so hurt. He was taking a bath when I brought up the subject. He started to cry which really unnerved me, and that put an end to that conversation. I felt sorry for him. And we got married. But there was more to my following through with the Roger thing. Why does 20/20 vision have to be "hindsight?!" I would have loved to have my wisdom gene turned on better in those days to guide my decisions.

Here was my twisted thinking. To reconcile the guilt I had for having an affair while I was married to Bob, I felt I had to legitimize that act by marrying Roger. As if to say, "See, I left for the right reason."

This is all quite painful to admit. But I promised frankness. So, we press on!

There I was, affair, new career, move into San Francisco, and husband number two.

We owned the recording studio together since the other partner left, and I ended up learning a lot about the commercial end of the business, including how to produce and edit audiotape. With a razor blade. Those were the days! I also started doing voice-over work, which was so much fun!

We built a good clientele of repeat customers, mostly advertising agencies. That was great because they had department store clients who had sales on a regular basis and needed TV and radio spots (commercials). Roger ran the recording sessions for the most part, and I ran the other company business setting session appointments, bookkeeping, liaising with clients and talent, and marketing.

As with any new business, we were consumed by our work. There wasn't time to sit back and relax because we had to be sure we were keeping the studio afloat. That's tough on a couple. I originally thought being together all the time would be great! But it wasn't such a great idea with this husband.

It took a while to recognize his overpowering possessiveness. At first, I liked the attention. I had felt a bit shunned by Bob and wanted more attention from him, but this new pendulum had swung way too far the other way. If Roger was working late at the studio, he would not let me go home, even though I had nothing to do and was exhausted. It wasn't worth fighting about, so, I'd sleep on the sound booth floor until we'd drive home together. I was suffocating. I felt like a prisoner. Why was he acting as if he didn't trust me? His behavior devolved into being wary around some of our male clients. His jealousy wasn't founded . . . at least at first.

The long hours and 24/7 focus on work and Roger's jealousy took their toll. Whatever romance we had at first was dissolving. That old familiar refrain repeated itself again. If I didn't feel madly in love, something was wrong. It must be over. I kept coming back to a core question, "Is there any such thing as true love?" I was determined to find the answer. Otherwise, why did I keep trying? How could I get a crush on a copywriter client who came to the studio on a regular basis to record some radio spots? Ah! This one was different, or so I thought at the time.

I hadn't yet learned that life, and the other people in our lives, are our mirrors. I had yet to see that the one common denominator in all these relationships was me!

Look out! Here comes number three!

Bill was … fun. Such a welcome energy in light of the cloud that had formed at work. He was naturally very romantic—a poet and a philosopher. He was also an extremely talented copywriter. He had a quick wit and great sense of humor, as you know, an important attribute for all my husbands!

He'd come to direct an audio session and then we'd leave to have long lunches where we talked about everything! At first, I fooled myself that this was part of maintaining good client relationships. But after several of these lunches, it was clearly about a powerful attraction.

I thought he was pretty perfect. Look up the definition of "infatuation."

Also, Bill was on a spiritual path so, while in the glow of that new relationship, I was inspired to get back into yoga. I had enjoyed my classes and meditations when I was in Geneva, and I wanted to do that again. I wanted to dive deeper into my spiritual self. I had always felt connected to God, the Universe, whatever you want to call it. I had had some amazing experiences when I was in nature—drug free peak experiences, and I wanted to find the secret to feeling that sense of connection and aliveness all the time.

I also wanted a relationship to be like that too—you know, "happily ever after." But Bill wasn't Prince Charming either. I'll explain that in more detail later.

I think my quest for a fairy tale was part of what drove me to these serial relationships, and there was a part of me that still could not fully believe that someone could love me "forever." I was a pretty cool person—outgoing, fun and funny, some talent and smarts. But I allowed my self-esteem to be overshadowed by the experiences of my childhood when I was not popular with the boys and was keenly aware of how I didn't measure up to my mother with her many suitors.

I wondered whether someone would want to stay with me for the long haul. Maybe they would find out something about me they didn't like and decide I wasn't enough. My lack of confidence outweighed my confidence. I think that's part of why I tended to leave relationships first—to save myself the pain of someone breaking up with me. I'd beat them to the punch.

CHAPTER 4
GREAT SCOTT!

And now to the other main character in my story.

I met Scott through the production company where we both worked in 1985. Cute. Fun. Alive! He was so talented and creative. When we had a few minutes, he would come and sit across from me at my desk and we would have the greatest philosophical conversations! I was practicing yoga, and Scott was very naturally spiritual. Oh! And of course, he also had the requisite sense of humor.

I said Scott was "cute." He didn't have the classic handsome looks that usually attracted me—like Bob and Bill. He was on the stocky side, but was in good shape. He was very fair-skinned with freckles everywhere. His eyes were a magnificent hazel color, shifting between sparkly blue and forest green for no apparent reason. Those gorgeous eyes were surrounded by some of the largest glasses I'd ever seen! But the glasses could not hide his dimples. Those dimples expressed glee and mischief both at the same time.

His hair was short and sandy colored with a mustache to match.

His hands were among my favorite features. Something

happened to me when I'd see him with a large TV camera on his shoulder, and I was smitten by the way his hand went up through a wide strap at the front of the camera to hold and adjust the lens. There was a pure artistry and grace that was palpable, even with that strong, masculine hand taming a large machine. I was mesmerized watching him.

And he had such command of his shooting, always looking for the best angle—held low to the ground for moving, dancing feet, or high overhead for the view from the top.

Yes, this was artistry, and I learned over time how much of an artist he was—in all media, in all things. He studied ceramics and sculpture and metal craft in high school; he was a writer at his core, he was an original, experimental cook, and he was an artist at communication and a master at romance.

We became good friends as we worked on projects together. I even became his coach for relationships. That's because I was experienced in romance and he was new. After all, he was, wait for it ... fourteen years younger.

I was married to Bill then, and Scott and Bill hit it off really well, too. Scott used to say that Bill reminded him of his father. Now there's a twist.

In the media production world, great friendships are born. When a crew works together over and over, you learn each other's rhythms, moods, the allowable length of time for throwing a fit, etc. If you work well together, if you care about each other, you have each other's backs. It's a team, a well-oiled machine.

Through many video and TV projects, my friendship with Scott grew. So, when his most recent relationship broke up, I decided to fix this great guy up with my stepdaughter.

You may hear me say more than once in this book, "Who says God doesn't have a sense of humor?!"

One weekend, Bill and I drove to UCLA from San Diego. We were going up to see a basketball game between UCLA and Oregon State. Yes, the Ducks. I invited Scott because Kelly would be there. Kelly was Bill's elder of two daughters, a cheerleader for the Ducks, and she'd be coming down to LA for the game. She and Scott could meet and they'd, well, you know, live happily ever after. That was not the case, however. He became a shoulder for Kelly to cry on about her recent break-up.

On the drive North, Scott talked in great detail about a pair of earrings he made for his then lady fair. They were in the shape of the yin/yang symbol. He designed them and made them from silver at the home of Gerhard, his high school art teacher and mentor who still lived up near Big Bear.

Scott was so articulate. I appreciated his gift of expression and his passion, just talking about earrings! I sat there that day beside Bill in the front seat of the car thinking, "I wish somebody loved me like that." If you had told me that I would actually end up with *that* somebody, I would have laughed out loud and told you to lay off the drugs. But there's God who also has a sense of humor! It wasn't until later that Scott revealed he fell in love with me the first day he saw me at the production company.

By 1985, Bill and I had split up. He had moved to Portland, Oregon, and I was renting a room in the house of a great lady in Encinitas, California. Fran and I hit it off from the start, and I was so lucky to find that haven with my dog, Mukti. Bill had not actually been a dog person. I adopted Mukti from the pound as a puppy, and he was mine without contention.

In fact, one day, Bill said to me, "It's me or the dog."

I said, "Thank you for making it easy for me!"

By the time I moved in with Fran, both Scott and I had moved on from the production company where we worked together. I was with another company and he was freelance. We hadn't seen each other for months.

Then one day, I heard Tom, the Production Manager, talking on the phone in our shared office. He was calling up freelance crew to hire for a video our company was producing.

It didn't take long before I figured out who Tom was talking to and said, "Is that Scott Madden?"

He said, "Yes."

So, I took the phone and we started bantering. It became playful and flirtatious quite quickly. SO flirtatious!

After the initial pleasantries of "how are you, what have you been doing?" I told Scott that Bill and I had split and I was waiting for the final divorce papers.

I thought he had quite the nerve when he said, "Well, Marce, if you ever need any, well, you know, physical attention, just let me know! No strings attached, of course." I was off my game with that one and completely blanked on a witty retort.

I know I was flushed and bug-eyed and silenced at that one. Phew! It's getting hot in here! In fact, when we hung up, the other people who were at our respective locations asked about what they heard because they felt the ring of fire themselves and wanted to check that what they heard at their end was for real.

But that is just a little preview of the beginning of us.

Our real beginning as a couple was to take place some months later when I got a phone call from Scott one Sunday afternoon, completely out of the blue.

He said, "I've just had one of the gnarliest (yes, he spoke Surferese) weekends of my life and you were part of it. Tonight will be a full moon. Do you want to go for a walk and I can tell you about it?"

I said, "Yes."

And he said, "I'll be there in a few hours."

We walked in the moonlight and he talked and talked. He talked about his wonderful family and childhood. The way he talked about his parents sounded so loving and respectful; I thought it was such a great sign of a healthy human being. One of the things he said that struck me most was, "I am the son of Jim and Judy Madden." He was proud of his heritage, proud of who he was. That sentence was so powerful.

Then he got around to telling me about his experience of that weekend.

He said, "I've had a couple DUI arrests and my sentence was to do a few days in jail in San Bernardino. It was gnarly because they don't separate the inmate populations there. You can have a misdemeanor and be in with rapists and murderers, and I was! Right there in a small holding cell with all of them. I wanted to disappear, be invisible."

I wasn't sure where this was going, but it did sound frightening to me.

He went on, "Maybe if I didn't draw their attention, they'd leave me alone. For the moment, they were busy forcing a guy who was down on his knees to crawl around the floor, quacking like a duck. I quietly moved off to a bench in the corner and visualized myself being *anywhere* but there! And then, there you were. You stood in front of me in a red kimono. Don't ask me how that came to me! But you looked beautiful and I was happy to dive into the distraction. I felt calm, and I just sat in that meditation until they came to let me out."

Scott told me it would take three hours to come to my

house because he called from a pay phone at the jail and had to drive straight from there to our moonlit walk.

We had tea and talked for hours more. His story touched and enthralled me. I was drawn to him. We were open and easy together. It scared me. This couldn't be happening. Up until this time, I was glad that I had not jumped out of one relationship into another, for a change. It had been months that I was on my own in Fran's house, and I know it was good for me. I was getting to know me better—my likes and dislikes, my rhythms, my interests, my friends, without being in a relationship; without someone else to adapt to, compromise with, make room for physically and mentally. Just me.

So, though the waves of attraction were turning intimate, I sent him home that night. It was happening too fast. Besides, I couldn't be *that* easy. Never on the first night ... (where did I get that?).

He came back the next night. After all, the moon was still full and we could go for another walk. Great conversation—family, philosophy. Amazing, a chatty, open guy. When does that ever happen? Uh oh. Was I falling? He's 14 years younger than I am! This could never work. Here we go again! Never say "never!"

Because I wasn't the only one falling.

And so it began. After having given up on Fairy Tale endings, I was cascading into one of my own.

Scott did spend the second night, and that was it—we never looked back. Whoops, I do need to be careful of the "never" word!.

The more I got to know Scott, the better he seemed. Passionate—about everything! Work, art, me ... and he talked so confidently and creatively about wanting to be a director. He was an enigma.

He told me how he turned in a high school essay

assignment in screenplay format. He got extra credit for doing that. He took class notes in the Lord of the Rings Elvish language, having painstakingly learned the symbols. Of course, that made it a bit hard when he had to go back to his notes to study for a test, but it sure was a cool idea at the time.

Scott's parents, Jim and Judy, moved to San Diego after they had grown up, met, and married in Brooklyn. Scott was born in San Diego and, within a few years, the family moved north to Crestline in the San Bernardino mountains.

When Scott told me he went to Rim of the World High School, I did not believe him. I could not believe there was a school of that name. But there was. And Scott excelled there mostly because of his mentor, Gerhard, and being able to take a massive amount of classes with him. They formed a bond that is unbreakable still.

Scott was a good student, good at sports, and had a strong cadre of friends.

That ability to make friends easily extended to his time in College after he had moved off the mountain to study Television and Film at San Diego State University. And the "tag team" was born—Chris, Kelly, Carol, Bob, Derek, Kenny, and Todd. A band of merry men (and one dynamic woman) who worked together and played together and drank together. The friendships were forged in their college production playground and continues to the present. Back then, Scott started a yearly ski trip with them that has lasted to this day ... sort of.

When we met at the Production Company, Scott was living with his three sisters in Del Mar. Their mother had died at a very early age some years before, and their dad was off with wife number two (I think Scott would insert "literally number two" here). Scott shared a room with one of his sisters. When we were at their apartment, I felt like I was back in college. No, that's not possible; I went to an all-women's college. Same with boarding school, for that matter. But the condition of the bedrooms was certainly similar.

Ah, school. A wealth of experiences in those years!

So, before we get into the fourth husband in this "march," join me in my time machine for a trip back in time.

CHAPTER 5
WHAT I LEARNED ABOUT IN SCHOOL

I went to Dana Hall, an all girls' boarding school in Wellesley, Massachusetts, for three years. Not much girl/boy experience under my belt in those years! Just the occasional dance with various boys' schools around New England, and rumors of saltpeter in our food to help keep us on the straight and narrow. Chaperones would wade among us to be sure our bodies were a few inches apart as we danced.

In order to go to a dance, you had to sign up ahead of time and hope you made the list. You'd sign your name with your height in two-inch heels. That way, you could be paired up with someone who would be about the right height for you. Sometimes.

I remember one dance in particular that was especially painful. First of all, we girls were bussed to this school, and it was miles away in another state. The bus trip took hours, and it was the dead of winter.

So, dressed up and made up, and wearing our two inch-heels, we talked and laughed and dozed as the bus wended its way through the snow-coated New England roads. The boy's school was in a remote location, so the populated areas grew more and more sparse. In the fading light of day, we could gaze out the bus windows and watch as open fields and dark woods would slideshow by.

When we turned up the drive to the school, it looked like we'd dropped back in time. The main building was right out of a horror movie, looming over us with spires and giant arched church windows. I could swear there were gargoyles, but I'm sure I'm embellishing the memory.

The bus doors squealed open and the winter air blasted in. We climbed out in our party dresses and shoes. Girls wore the shoes they wanted! Some tall girls wore flats, and some sported heels higher than the "sign up" 2-inchers. I was 5'8", which was tall in those days, so I didn't need to make myself any taller. You know, boys mature later than girls. I didn't like dancing with guys who are shorter.

We trekked across the packed snow covering the ground to the massive stone steps up to the main building. We were greeted at the door by a couple of monitors, and escorted upstairs where we could freshen up and then be introduced to our dates.

When the time came to meet our dates for the first time, we went out to the landing at the top of the stairs. It was a long, sweeping, elegant staircase.

The batch of boys waited at the bottom. One at a time, our names were loudly read off a list. A student from our school would read the girls' names, and a student from their school would read the name of the boy we'd been matched with. When our name was called, we each descended that endless, *Gone With the Wind* staircase, and we wouldn't know who our date was until he stepped forward from the crowd when we got to the bottom. But that's not the worst of it. As each girl took her solo flight, the boys below would either whistle or boo, depending on where you fell on their approval scale. I'm not kidding! And if you don't think I was panicked that I'd catch a heel on the step or otherwise pull a pratfall, then you've never been embarrassed in front of a crowd.

Healthy groundwork for developing good relationships with the opposite sex, right? I will never erase that scene from my mind. Luckily, I didn't get booed. I didn't get a rousing cheer, either. But as I look back on my younger years to examine how I learned about love and relationships, I see these flashbacks of moments where the messages I got were, well, pretty screwed up! "Four boys and one's a girl" was only the beginning.

That dance night was just one of many experiences of my time at Dana. There were many more during those three years. But there's one more in particular that I want to tell you about. I think it is pertinent to the theme of this book, and has etched itself very deeply into my memory. And this is when I received a foreshadowing of things to come.

I went to boarding school because it's what most of my friends did, and it was also a family tradition. Both my parents had gone to boarding school as well as my two older brothers. Besides, the local high school was more about big hair and switchblades and that unforgettable Massachusetts accent, than education.

My brothers had the unfortunate fate of being expected to follow in my father's footsteps and go to the same school as he and his brothers and father and uncles. There were some advantages to being an only girl! My mother went to eight different schools by the time she was done, and didn't have loyalty to any of them, so no pressure there for me on the girl side of the equation. But eight schools? Yes. She was a good student, but managed to get kicked out or leave for a variety of reasons—like getting caught smoking one night on the roof of her dorm.

I knew lots of kids my age who wanted to go away to school to get away from home. It wasn't like that for me. I loved my family and liked being home. I was devastatingly home sick in my first months away. I enrolled as a sophomore, having completed 9th grade at Applewild where I'd been since the 4th grade. I knew all the teachers and most all the other kids, and was also well known myself. I was captain of one of our two sports teams, a good student, member of the drama and glee clubs ... I had a strong sense of self and confidence. Not a great hit with the boys, except as a friend, but otherwise relatively popular.

That all melted at boarding school because I was starting from scratch. I knew only a few of the girls, but was otherwise a blank slate. I'd have to prove myself anew at every turn—in the classroom and on the playing field. What? Try out for a sport? But didn't they know I was varsity? No such luck. Until later, that is, when I became captain of one of the Dana school teams! Ha!

So, yes, I was homesick. I missed knowing where I belonged, what I was good at, and the acknowledgement from faculty, friends, and family who also knew me and what I was good at. I felt blue all the time. I'd sit in study hall at night and just stew and fret, constantly on the verge of tears. Because no one there knew me or who I was, I felt like I didn't know me, not like at Applewild. I was now proving myself again—including to me.

I had a sweet roommate, Priscilla. We were in a small house on campus. The school was ancient! There were some old dorm buildings from the 1800's, but girls were otherwise housed in what were once neighborhood homes. Ours was a small one that only housed about 13 girls. As I said, Priscilla was a dear person, but she didn't hang out in our room much, choosing to go visit other girls upstairs. I felt quite left out and shunned by my housemates. I couldn't help feeling that something was off, which only added to my sense of separation and loneliness, though that was getting better as I found new footing in my classes and sports. I wondered if I'd maybe inadvertently done something wrong, pissed somebody off or something. So, one day, I sat Priscilla down and just came out and asked her if there was something I needed to know or do to set things right with the girls in the house.

She said, "Well, yes, there is something … some of the girls say you're a lesbian."

I was stunned! Didn't see that one coming. "Oh my God! No! Really?! … What's a lesbian?"

I honestly had no idea. I guess I seemed weird to them because I'd been keeping to myself and was awkward in their presence. These girls were different from me. I truly didn't know how to be around them. Several of them were really beautiful and they did stuff I couldn't relate to. For example, they wore curlers to bed every night and put on make-up in the morning. I had had my share of sleeping in curlers before I went to Dana, but that's because I wanted to look attractive to the boys. This was an all-girls' school. Why did they care? For me to be free of those tubular head torture devices was just fine. Besides, curling my hair at night and sleeping on curlers never worked for me anyway. My hair was so thick, it still would be soaking wet in the morning. Lost cause. I just didn't have those girlie skills of knowing how to do my hair or put on make-up. I'd watch my mother do it almost every morning in front of her vanity, but she didn't teach me anything about how to do it myself.

She also hadn't given me any of the girls boarding school warnings that other girls got from their mothers: that there would be *those* girls who might be interested in them physically and to be on the look-out. Of course! Those dreadful lesbians. Now I knew what the word meant because, it's somewhat embarrassing to admit, I had to look it up in the dictionary. Wow, try it sometime! For a girl who knew nothing about sex in the first place, short of enjoying when a boy would hold me close when we danced and I could feel his ... interest, this was a real eye-opener! The description turned my sense of reality on its head.

Like I said, "foreshadowing."

It took me quite a while to be around the other girls in the house again without them looking at me askance. They finally relaxed and accepted me, but that experience scarred my quite deeply. Obviously, it's still very fresh in my memory. It added to my self-questioning. Who was I? What vibe did I give off in the first place for them to draw that conclusion? I had a taste of what it's like to be mistaken for something you're not. You get treated differently, you get treated *as* different, you can be marginalized or even shunned. It's unsettling to be treated in a certain way because of a label that has been erroneously stuck to you. I was able to fix that. What if you couldn't?

I didn't discover until many years later how close to home being called a lesbian had hit!

I promised to get to the Scott love story—to the be all, end all of love stories, and my marriage number four. But I think it's valuable to share a few pertinent facts about some of my early relationships that didn't end in marriage but that added to my love learning curve.

CHAPTER 6
THE BEST PART ABOUT THE PAST IS THAT IT'S BEHIND YOU!

I had an inferiority complex starting in elementary school ... at least about the boy thing. Why? Here are a few theories.

My parents were good at telling me that I was beautiful, but I had trouble believing them. After all, they were my parents, they were supposed to think that.

I always felt like I was overweight and didn't know how to get it under control. I wasn't that heavy, but the point is that I felt I was. My mother was heavy when she was a teenager and, when I asked her how she lost the weight, she said her father would always rap her knuckles with his butter knife any time he saw her reaching for the butter. That didn't help me with my issue. Eventually, I lost touch with my appetite, so I didn't stop eating because I felt full, I just kept going. And I envied people who could stop eating even before cleaning their plate because they felt full. I wished for that feeling.

It probably didn't help that one of my brothers nicknamed me "thunder thighs." Cute, huh? He's a character and loves to joke around, often not fully aware of how a funny line might land. He wasn't being malicious. Hurt just the same. I still remind him of it!

All this started an adversarial relationship with the scale that exists to this day, even though my doctor now tells me to gain a few pounds! Now that's advice I'd craved most of my life, even the times I had managed to lose weight on a crash diet.

I think there's also something to that comment of my mother's that she has "four boys and one's a girl." We siblings all look like my father. That made me feel boyish; I didn't see myself as a girlie girl at all. I was a tomboy who wasn't afraid to climb trees and get dirty, and would much rather wear jeans or my cowgirl outfit that be in a dress.

I remember asking my mother one day if I was adopted (isn't that a typical kid's question?).

Her answer was, "Are you kidding? Look around you. If anyone in this family is adopted, it's me!"

I had great friendships in elementary school but, when my friends seemed to be pairing up boy/girl, I was left out of that equation. I was either snowed over some boy who didn't return my feelings, or some boy was interested in me, but I didn't return his feelings.

So, I didn't feel popular with boys. They could be friends, sure; boyfriend, no.

In truth, I think I was also always measuring myself against my mother. In her day, she was the belle of every ball. She had beaus galore and I've read the love letters to prove it. She was beautiful, vivacious, smart, and funny as a whip. She could sing and dance and play the piano. At Christmastime, we would gather around the piano while she would play Christmas Carols, with her long, painted nails clicking on the keys, and sing along with her beautiful voice. When she'd go to dances as a young woman, she'd get invited up by the band to sing with them. She was also fearless! She made a name for herself wherever she went. When she got into politics, she was Chairman of the Republican City Committee in Fitchburg, and also was a delegate to the Convention in 1956. She knew top politicians and statesman, and they knew her, including Richard Nixon. I won't comment on politics at this juncture.

Even though Mummy was a Republican, she invited Eleanor Roosevelt to come to Fitchburg to speak to a women's organization. And she came! Not only that, she stayed in our house and apparently bounced me on her knee! Wish I could remember that. Sometimes I think I do, but it's also easy to create a memory from what we've heard.

My mother was a master at asserting herself. She once went to a car race with another couple. The husband owned a BMW sports car he planned to enter in the race. Somehow, it was my mother who ended up behind the wheel, competing against an all-male track, and she won. Of course she did!

Naturally, she also did well in school. Oh, and she was a ribbon-winning horse woman.

Mic drop.

How could I live up to any of that? I loved singing, and would dance and fly around the house singing along with the soundtracks of West Side Story and Gypsy. She heard me one day and said, "You can't carry a tune in a paper bag." I have never, never forgotten that. It cut deep. Anything I did that she had done, she did better—field hockey, jumping horses ... everything. I sucked at my piano lessons and quit after a few weeks. Yes, I fed my own insecurities, but she did do a few things to help, as you can see.

She wasn't a witch. She was a good mother. Good

instincts; quick to act when any of us got hurt. But I was the only daughter. I think she was a bit wound up in wanting to train me to be a good woman, but maybe there was a touch of jealousy on her part, too. I was starting out, and my whole life was ahead of me. Her life was on the down slope of aging. I don't think she could bear that. That took me years to surmise.

After my three years at Dana Hall, and those awkward, unreal dances, I went on to Bennett College.

During boarding school and college, I used to sneak out of school to visit brother number two, Morgan, in Vermont where he was a ski instructor. What could be a better set up? It was the '60s. Free love. Rock and roll and folk songs. And my brother was known everywhere! We resemble each other enough that people could take one look at me and ask if I was Morgan's sister, even when he wasn't around. But they knew him well enough. That got me through a lot of doors and ski lifts.

Anyway, a band used to play in one of Morgan's regular evening hangouts where he was the bouncer. I hit it off with the drummer. Sucker for drummers, gotta say!

One night, he and I went back to my brother's trailer where I was staying and "it" happened. Wait, what? Is that all there is? Is this what I was saving myself for? Is this the thing my mother told me she would disown me over? Really?

There it was. In 1968, I "lost my virginity" at the age of 19. Lost? Why *do* we say that? It's not as if we could ever find it again, or someone would say to you, "Don't worry, Honey, you can replace it."

In retrospect, it was a fine first time. I didn't have a chance to get nervous. And how in the *Hell* do people "do it" when they've had no instruction? Who said God doesn't have a sense of humor? You do what? Luckily, Freddie was experienced and gave me coaching. I'm sorry, but learning to ride a bike was much easier.

The next day after Freddie had left, I went running into my brother's bedroom in the trailer where my friend Leah was sleeping in. I ran in a bit panicked. Oh no! I crossed the line, my mother would be able to tell … what was I going to do? As I ran to tell Leah, I was already shouting, "Leah, Leah! I'm not a virgin anymore!" She sat up in bed and said, "Yay!" OK, well that changed the whole tone of the moment. I thought, "Yeah, Yay! The chastity belt was gone and I stepped into womanhood." That response from Leah probably saved me. It completely interrupted and turned around the thought road I was starting to go down and made me feel everything was all right.

So that relationship went on for a while. I'd go to the bar where Morgan worked and Freddie's group played. I still remember how one night Freddie sang the old song "That's All" to me in the crowded club. What woman wouldn't swoon? His nickname for me was "Mush Mouse." We girls will answer to anything! I loved playing grown-up. It was a fun combo of naughty and new doors flying open.

But after some months, I started wondering if this was the real thing. I questioned if I knew whether this was love, and I was heading off to Europe that spring for a third year abroad. Because of the program I majored in at Bennett, I'd studied secretarial practice and French, and was hired for a position in the World Alliance of YMCAs in Geneva, Switzerland.

At 20, I was on my own in a foreign country for a year. The geographical distance contributed to my feeling of distance from Freddie. So much so that, when he said he'd come to Europe to be with me, I told him not to. I felt my blood go cold when he made the offer, so I knew something wasn't right. I knew he would not fit in with my new life … that he was not a fit for me. I had a new job, new friends, new experiences and I was more independent than ever—out of reach of my old life, my parents, my former me.

After a few weeks of exploring the city of Geneva, I found a café that I really liked. I went there on a Sunday, and discovered it is the place to go for a Swiss soccer team after a practice or local game. They were all cute and chatty and loved testing this American girl's French. They knew no English except lyrics from songs or some basic pleasantries and jokes. My French had been pretty good in a formal setting, but these guys often cracked up at some of my more archaic phrases that I'd learned in school. I'd say something and they'd say, "Quoi?" several times before one of them caught on, told the others, and they broke into gales of laughter. Then they'd explain my faux pas and instruct me on how that would be said in this generation.

I told my female friends about this find, and quite quickly, Sunday mornings at this café was the destination for us as well as the soccer team. Let's just say, this was a great impetus for us to practice our French while they could also learn English. All of us were in need of learning the more colloquial language than the text book version.

There was one particular team member, Danny, who caught my eye with his wide, crinkly smile and twinkling brown eyes. I apparently caught his eye, too, and we started seeing each other. Wow! That strikes me as a really weird wording!

So now I had a new Swiss-French boyfriend, and my mind and heart were that much further from Freddie. Naturally, Freddie and I had talked about getting back together when I returned to the states, but we both knew that wouldn't happen. He didn't want to give up on us, but he saw the inevitable and gradually accepted that we were no longer an "us."

So, sexual relationship number two. On the first night I spent at Danny's place, I woke up the next morning to breakfast with his family! He lived with his father and two brothers. They all smiled knowingly at both of us as we entered the kitchen. Eeeeek! I couldn't imagine this happening at home, and yet they seemed quite comfortable. In fact, if I read the signals right, they also looked pleased that Danny had bagged an American girl. Sounds harsh, but we did see less of each other after that.

Geneva is so beautiful, and so rich in culture. Our World Alliance office was completely diverse, since this was the world headquarters for the YMCA. I enjoyed being thought of as the resident hippie. You know, I was their token American, and that was all it took. They saw the news and the stories about America in the '60s, so they just assumed. But the USA was not particularly popular with the rest of the world back then, and I was not proud to be an American. It was Nixon and Vietnam, and Charlie Manson, and Europe was not our biggest fan.

Actually, I enjoyed when people couldn't tell I was American and miss-took me for another nationality. One person told me I spoke French with a Swedish accent! I don't know how I managed that, but it was OK with me.

Soon after my arrival in Geneva, I signed up for a yoga class. I took the class because it was in French, and was a good excuse to say I was furthering my education in the language. I was also learning yoga—something that would be part of my life from then on.

Ah, and then there was my yoga teacher, Robert.

He was so handsome, in a Yul Brenner way—only better. He was half Austrian and half Italian. Hello!

He didn't understand why a young woman like me

would be interested in yoga. He usually saw people come to class because they were older and making a last ditch effort to get healthy.

He'd invite me for tea after our weekly class, and we'd talk. He was so much older. But I had a crush. I loved our discussions about life and yoga and spirituality. I realized maybe I'd told him too much about my life when I shared how I was overweight as a teen and my brother called me "thunder thighs."

There we were, first night of headstands. He was going around helping the other students, speaking to them, coaching them in French in a whisper. When he got to me, he bent down and whispered in my ear, "get those thunder thighs up there!" That's what I got for sharing that awful nickname my brother had given me years before. But the sting of those words melted. Now, it was our little joke, and I liked my yoga teacher all the more.

One night, after weeks of yoga classes, we agreed to meet at a restaurant. I wanted him to meet Leah who was in town as part of a European trip. At some point in the evening, I got the feeling that he liked me—more than as teacher/student. It was something I'd fantasized about but, once it seemed truly reciprocated, it felt creepy. Ew! I did not like the feeling at all, and he fell right off the pedestal. My guru had become too human and I could not reconcile the two feelings.

New feelings were swirling around me. Questions continued to play in my mind.

I had a couple more crushes while I was in Geneva, but I still didn't understand love yet. I did feel good about having spent a year abroad on my own, getting fluent in French, fending for myself, and surviving quite well.

By the time my year was up and I came home to the states, my parents had moved to Marin County, California.

I took off cross-country to *visit* my family in Pumpkin, the Fiat 124 Sport Coupe of that color that my Dad let me buy in Switzerland and ship home.

I loved Pumpkin! OK, one more Geneva story. It's not a relationship story, but it does add another dimension to the way in which my mother contributed to my confusion.

When I lived in Switzerland, two friends and I drove to Italy for the Christmas holiday. Driving meant we had to go over Mont Blanc between the two countries. It was snowing like a bandit, and it was late in the day when we got to the base of the mountain. Officials were encouraging people not to try the drive over because cars were getting stuck. But I had Pumpkin, good New England winter driving experience, and two passengers who were game, so we went for it. OK, I admit, it was cool to see both sides of the road littered with the stalled-out cars that couldn't make it and had slid off into the snowbanks. But I had the little Pumpkin that could, and we all cheered as we got to the top and were ready to descend on the other side.

See, it was my mother who taught me how to drive ... because she wanted to be sure I would not "drive like a girl." That was the same training she'd gotten from her father. Just a reminder here that it's a good idea to take a look at the messages we get, especially early in life. What might be a casual remark can have a lasting effect on us. More on this later.

You've probably guessed that my "visit" to California was a complete relocation.

My next ten years in the Bay Area could be a book. It was the '60s. That's telling in itself. No, I didn't do drugs, but I lived with a dealer. You know, the more I look back at what was happening in my life, the more I might just be seeing a pattern! Contradictions, opposites, ironies, yins and yangs....

I did the waitress thing for a few months—lunches by day; cocktails by night. I had to really know drinks, because I would take orders from customers, rearrange them in my head by the liquor in them, and order them that way to the bartender. I still remember it—bourbon, scotch, gin, vodka, rum, brandy, wines and beers. So, I could get a gin martini order from one table and a gin and tonic from another, and had to order them together. Then I had to remember where they went and what the prices were so I could charge the customers at their respective tables. Oh yeah, and we weren't allowed to write anything down.

There was one night when I was serving a table of ten and they all had really complicated, frou-frou drinks.

As I was taking the order, one of the men at the table said, "Don't you want to be writing this down?"

And I said, "No thanks, I got it." And sure enough!

So, I went to order the drinks, got the order perfect, prices and proper change and all. That was a landmark for me. But then, I went back to their table later to see if they wanted anything else, and the same man said they wanted another round, and started to point out who had what. I said, "That's OK, I remember," and I did! They were blown away and I got a great tip. I also decided I could now quit the cocktailing part of the job. I crossed a threshold.

One day soon after, I was serving lunch to a psychiatrist who came in quite often. My mother went to him a few times, so I knew him pretty well. We had become friends and I always loved any time with him. He had a build and a jolliness like Santa Claus, and he was wise, erudite and open-minded.

As I set his burger on the table, I said, "If you ever need any help in your office, let me know."

He said, "Call me tomorrow; my secretary is retiring."

That started a string of a few years working for several different shrinks, first in Kentfield with Dr. Lamers and six others, then in Mill Valley for a psychiatrist and a psychologist. It's good for Marin to have a plentiful supply!

During these years, I had a few relationships along the way. Let's see, a gay man who I thought I could "turn" (I know, I know!), an abusive man whom I believed when he said he would never hit me again after that first time. Don't ever believe that. No need to list any others.

Suffice to say, I sure knew how to pick 'em!

Then came the husband parade of Bob, Roger, and Bill.

CHAPTER 7
LOOKING FOR LOVE IN ALL THE WRONG PLACES-OUTSIDE!

You already know those three marriages didn't survive. I especially wanted the third one with Bill to make it. I wanted to know what love was, what commitment was. I had flunked that test too often and needed to see at least this one through.

I want to inspect that relationship with you more closely before our Scott story continues. I discovered there were more lessons to learn about myself in that marriage, and some of them turned out to be pivotal.

Bill and I were married for about eight years. A record for me. But, as hopeful as I was to really make it all the way this time, this was ultimately not to be.

Though Bill and I had met in San Francisco and got together there, we ended up moving to Oregon. His family was there (one of his ex-wives, and his two daughters, brother and his family, and his mom, until she passed). There were also many old friends, some of whom were more than friends. Don't get me started. I was up against quite a history.

There was a company in Portland that was wooing him

to come work for them.

Husband number two, Roger, had walked away from the recording studio in San Francisco, leaving it to me. I was going to Portland with Bill, so I left the company to my brother who had already been working for us. Doug had learned to be quite the engineer and businessman.

Off to Portland from San Francisco. Ah, I thought it was great—the climate and architecture reminded me so much of the East Coast, I felt at home to some extent. I got a job at a film production house running their little audio studio and had a blast! I was to work on the sound for films and AV presentations they created and I was also expected to bring in my own clients for audio projects, which I did. Had a great run at Odyssey Productions.

While we were in Portland, I loved listening to Dr. David Viscott on the radio. Oh my God! A caller would go on the air and describe their issue, and Dr. Viscott would say something to them that sounded off the subject they raised, and completely out of the blue. But, inevitably, that person would start to cry or gasp in amazement. David hit the nail on the head—over and over again—always getting to the heart of the real issue in one minute's time. I loved him. I loved how direct and clear and sharp he was. I loved that he helped people. There was one breakthrough another. So, I swore that, if I ever wanted to talk to a therapist, he'd be it. But he was all the way in LA. Oh well.

It turned out that our Portland days were numbered.

After a few years there, Bill and I got invited to move to San Diego to work for a televangelist who had a popular TV show in syndication, and we were to be the promo team.

Well, honestly, I didn't care much who we might be working for. We traveled from Portland, Oregon, which was sitting in a sheath of ice in March, to San Diego,

California. Clincher, thank you! Are you kidding? Beach? Warm weather? Palm trees? The Portland gilt was definitely off the lily.

We got the job and moved to Cardiff-By-The-Sea in North County San Diego. How could we resist with a name like that? The area was so beautiful, and the drive was pretty easy from there to the Ministry's office in an old estate in La Jolla.

It turned out that the people who worked in the ministry for the televangelist were steeped in EST, short for Erhard Sensitivity Training.

Here's a diversion story that relates to the EST subject.

When I first moved to Northern California from the East Coast, my first job was in San Francisco. This was before I worked in the restaurant in Marin. The San Francisco business was a children's encyclopedia sales company. The company only hired young women to go door to door selling sets of the encyclopedias.

The head of our office, which was located over Finocchio's, a bar in San Francisco which featured female impersonators as the entertainment. (I hear you chuckling again), was Werner Erhard.

Yes, the mastermind behind EST was the consummate salesman who taught me how to knock on doors: "Hi, My name is Marcy. I've been asked to call on the mothers in the neighborhood. This is my letter of introduction. May I step in?"

I quit as soon as I sold a set of encyclopedias. I couldn't stand the job. The day I said I wanted to quit, Werner himself spent a lot of time with me, trying to talk me into staying. Wow! They brought in the big guns! Suffice to say, he is a very persuasive guy. However, that did not deter me. What was weird was that I was very emotional! Here I was, crying up a storm in the meeting and not knowing why. It made me question whether I was OK. I was so tired and I had a sore throat without the other cold symptoms. I also had a mild fever and throbbing headache. In those days, I used the *Well Body Book* as my health bible. I looked up my symptoms and saw they could indicate Mononucleosis. So, I found a doctor and went to him saying, "I think I have Mono."

He patronizingly said, "Well, let's not get ahead of ourselves. Let's do some tests."

The doctor called the next day and said, "You were right!" Great, Mono. At least that explained my over the top emotional reaction to leaving the encyclopedia sales job.

That was the late '60s.

Fast forward to 1984 and back to the job at the ministry. There Bill and I were, dropped into a community of EST graduates. I was never interested in doing EST, though it was all the rage back then. After all, I had learned sales from Werner almost 20 years before. But I did end up taking the training in self-defense once we'd been at the ministry for about a month. I say "self-defense" because all the language people used in the office was obviously right out of EST. Werner had invented a language all its own. For example, you don't talk about being mad about something; a person is "plugged in." Now, I happen to believe that we have a very good language already. We have a word for everything! So why go around reinventing when the original model is working fine?

Oh, and in this ministry which was also based on Science of Mind as well as EST, be careful not to ever complain about anything because you create your own world with your mind, and if something is not going right, you'll be asked, "What is it within you that created that?"

The philosophy of how we create our own world with

our minds is meant as a personal contemplation to lead to self-discovery and growth. It should not be used as a weapon to put down others. Unfortunately, I saw that happening all too often with the ministry staff.

There was the day I went to the kitchen to get a cup of coffee and two women were in there having a fairly heated exchange that went something like this:

Woman 1: "What is it within you that you are late getting your monthly report to me every time?"

Woman 2: "Well, what is it within you that always makes me late with my reports?"

That did it! Really? Nothing like a little blame under the guise of taking responsibility.

For the record, I do believe in the power of the mind and the myriad ways we create our experience of life. What I could not abide at the ministry, and with EST, was that those teachings were delivered like they were sharp knives stabbing at the person being addressed. There was no love. You had to bludgeon the ego before it would step aside to allow the spiritual Self to emerge. However, there are spiritual paths that show us the way to recognize our ego, to rally our minds to serve us, to live to our spiritual potential by using love.

Bill and I worked at the ministry for a few months. After about six months, Bill decided to go on his own as a freelance copywriter. I stayed at the ministry for a total of nine months until I just had to leave, too. They had gone through a reorganization and the broadcast part of promotion was moved under another department. How would you feel if you were introduced to your new supervisor whose first words were, "Women really win in my space?" I quit right then and started looking for what was next. It didn't take long to find out.

Within a couple months, Bill was talking about leaving

me. He was restless, I guess, and I think he missed his old life in Portland. I was his third marriage, so he didn't have a great track record either—no poster child for commitment. We were puttering along, but things had not been ideal. Sexual connection was non-existent, and pretty much had been from the start. Bill had … let's just say a "challenge" functioning. By now you might have assumed that I took that as a challenge. Of course I could fix that—I could be the one. Oy. What is it within me?

There we were. The tables had turned. There was a part of me that looked at this as getting my just karma since, this time, someone was leaving me. Ah, turn-about. It's always there! It's been said that it doesn't matter if you believe in karma; karma believes in you.

I suggested counseling. This time, I wanted to work at the marriage. This time, I was determined to know what love is, what commitment is, once and for all.

Naturally, my first thought of a counselor was Dr. Viscott. Since we had moved to San Diego, he was now just up the road in LA! So, I pulled out an LA phone book (no Google in those days) and found a phone number for Dr. David Viscott. I assumed that I'd be calling his institute, because he had established an organization to teach other therapists the "Viscott Method." But, when I called, I recognized that familiar voice from the radio shows I'd listened to in Portland.

I was so shocked that he answered the phone himself that I said, "Oh Wow! I got the horse's mouth!"

He chuckled and said, "I've been called a lot of things in my day …" and he asked why I was calling.

I gave the crib notes on the situation with Bill, and he explained that he was not taking private clients anymore and to please call the Institute. He wished me luck and gave me the number.

When I called, the woman who answered said "Is this Marcy?"

Taken aback, I said, "Yes."

She said that David had just called and asked her to let me know that he'd changed his mind and did want to see Bill and me after all.

We had two sessions and, true to what I remembered of Dr. Viscott, he cut to the chase, well, after a while, that is. At first, it felt like we were just having an expensive, mundane chat, and I was getting impatient. But, within a few minutes, he asked Bill a question that prompted Bill to admit he'd stepped out on me a few times. Wait, "stepped out?" Shit! He cheated on me!

I thought this would be the most dreaded thing I could ever imagine but, when David asked how I felt about hearing that news, I surprised even myself by saying that I was relieved! What?

He said, "Do you know why you feel relieved?"

I laughed and said, "I have no idea!"

He said, "It's because you now know that you can trust your instincts. There was a part of you that knew this all along, and now you can be confident in your intuition."

With those words, I felt like my wiring was reconnected. I felt strong. I was not so ready to be told that something was my imagination anymore. I could stand in my own beliefs.

Within a few months of our last session with Dr. Viscott, Bill and I did split. I had done the homework Dr. Viscott gave us, but Bill wasn't into it, and he still wanted to leave. I called Dr. Viscott in tears and he told me to ask Bill if he really had to go; could he stay awhile?

I was aghast. "Why would I want to be with anyone who didn't want to be with me?"

Dr. Viscott told me, "You have to get to the bottom of

why your relationships went this way. I'm frankly not convinced that Bill is 'the one' for you, but until you figure out what this is all about, you're destined to keep repeating the pattern."

I asked Bill to stay. He agreed, but in a month's time, he announced again he wanted to leave. He had a job offer in Portland he wanted to pursue. And he wanted to go alone. That was that.

I had a brand new experience from this, a break in my pattern. This time, I felt confident that I had worked at the marriage—really worked at finding what it would take for a couple to stay together, even when a spouse breaks a most important vow. At last, I knew what commitment felt like. Though we couldn't save the marriage, I did achieve the goal of knowing commitment at least. I wasn't the one to leave; he was.

When we did agree to part ways, it felt … done. I felt good that I had made every effort I could, and I felt ready to move on with my life.

In that moment, I made a promise to myself that, if I was to be with someone again, they needed to love me as much as I loved them, and that I could no longer seek fulfillment in another. I had to learn how to love myself.

CHAPTER 8
FULL CIRCLE

Here we are. Divorce number three. This is where Scott re-enters the picture. Yes, after sending him home that first night when we walked and talked under the light of the full moon, that was it. I didn't send him home ever again.

Though he was much younger, he had a maturity that went beyond his years. He had a strong grasp of human nature and was constantly making insightful observations about people, somehow tapping into a deep sense of knowing. He loved to talk (nice change in a guy), and about anything—philosophy, art, film, cooking, and relationship, and he was well versed in all of them. He was positive and confident—as if "insecurity" was not in his vocabulary.

We did everything together, went everywhere together. We hated being apart for even the shortest stretch of time. He would travel for work, but I would join him on a couple of the locations. We also often got hired on the same projects.

In San Diego production, you had to be able to wear many hats to survive. There were not too many specialists who survived on doing one thing. You could be a director one day, a gaffer the next, the audio person or craft services another day!

There was one memorable project we worked on together in 1988 that I want to tell you about because it was a special time for both of us. It was our first time working outside the country together, and it brought us closer. We had to be more on our toes, more in sync, and ready for experiences and encounters that would be nothing like what we were used to at home.

The project took us to the Soviet Union (yes, it was called that at the time) with a group of U.S. citizens to videotape their meetings with designated counterparts from the Soviet Union. They were there to discuss human rights.

Scott had been working on another project intended to give the Jewish response to "Beyond War." The man who hired him was Rabbi Shelly Moss. Scott would go to Shelly's house to discuss the video, and they struck up a connection right away. Scott would come home raving about what an amazing man Shelly was—such an inspiration, such deep understanding and caring and downright brilliance. All in this warm, gentle package.

One day, out of the blue in one of their meetings, Shelly asked Scott if he'd like to go to the Soviet Union. They talked about it and Scott accepted with the stipulation that I come, too. He and I were the entire crew. Camera, lights, audio and grips. We lugged our own equipment around and handled all aspects of the shoot.

There we were, in Moscow in December. It was cold and snowy and beautiful—a magical and eye-opening time.

Moscow bustled like any big city. Cars and people everywhere. The women were all dressed in stylish boots and fur coats and hats. The men had long, black overcoats and fur hats with flaps to cover their ears in the cold, bitter temperatures. I thought it would feel like a depressed country. It seemed anything but, at least in the parts we saw. Beautiful Georgian architecture which always sent a shock wave through me because the grand, clapboard buildings were often painted in yellow and pink and light greens and blues—colors you'd expect to see in Bermuda, the tropics, not in subzero, snow-covered Moscow.

During the day, we were to videotape the human rights meetings between the Russian and American representatives with each country to share their progress as well as to take responsibility for their failures in that area. Interesting that the Americans spoke first and were quite candid about the atrocities of our country's past. When it was the Russians' turn, they had a way of explaining their past in a way that bespoke no wrong-doing.

The meetings were held in a large conference room at the "Peace Committee." Everyone was seated on the outside of a square made by four long, narrow tables.

The entire middle area was open, and that's where Scott and the camera were stationed. That way, he could swing in all directions to record the person speaking. Each participant had an infrared translation device with earphones so they could receive simultaneous translation.

I was set up outside the square, behind a participant. I had extra batteries and videotapes to slide to Scott across the carpeted floor when he needed them. We'd worked out hand signals for that. He'd slide the shot cassettes back to me so I could number and label them.

There he was, literally at the center of this historic show. Unruffled, master of his domain. There was that shooting stance I'd fallen in love with—strong hand on the camera lens, feet apart to ensure balance, and knees somewhat bent as if he was going into battle. And his strong back, widest at the shoulders. A shape I thought I would never grow tired of.

His sandy, reddish hair was longer now, and his glasses

in much better proportion to his face than the goggles he wore in the early days.

I loved watching Scott in the evening meetings we had with the esteemed U.S. participants who got together to debrief the day. He was always able to speak up boldly, even when his remarks or observations might be seen as fiery or even contentious. But he always had a perspective that enriched the conversation and often lent the key ingredient to deciding how the next day should go.

He moved about this strange land with ease and calm.

One day, we decided to go out to shoot some "B roll" so we'd have plenty of images to edit into whatever this video was to become.

There we were in Red Square on one of the coldest of those December days ... we even had some fresh snowfall. The Kremlin was to the right, and St. Basil's Cathedral was before us with its pointed spires and multi-colored onion domes defying the gray skies behind them. The cathedral demands respect and awe in spite of the fact that it looks like something out of Willy Wonka—a building made of sweet tempting candies.

We got some amazing footage that day, and loved wandering on our own, not always knowing where we were or where we were going. At one point, a lone street vendor opened up his greatcoat in front of us to reveal an assortment of fur hats attached to the lining. He was quite pushy as I tried to let him know I wouldn't be interested. It finally took my exclaiming, "I don't want to wear a dead animal on my head!" He knew enough English to move away cautiously. Scott and I laughed for blocks! We also marveled at how we managed to get directions to the art district, Arbot Street, from a woman who was pushing her beautiful, bundled-up, rosy-cheeked baby in a carriage. It wasn't until we walked away in the direction she sent us that we realized the whole exchange had taken place with sign language, facial expressions and finger maps in the snow, no words. A lesson in cross cultural communication.

Even as we wandered, it was clear Scott always had a sense of direction. When we decided to take a subway back toward our hotel, he navigated the stations and the Cyrillic signs as if he knew the language. He made me feel safe, protected. And all along, he had to protect the huge video camera as well. He got incensed when we would head through the doors to enter or exit a building because, if there were a man passing through in front of us, they would never hold the door, and would let it close in my face. Scott would confront them with a gesture or words. Some inflections are understandable in any language. He couldn't believe someone would be so rude to a woman. My hero!

Over a couple days during a lunch, we got talking with a great group of young Russian students associated with the Peace Committee. We went out with them a few times— once to an amazing, high class restaurant; once to the home of Alexei and his family.

Alexei was studying "American" at the University. No, he made it very clear, he was learning American, not English. Imagine his joy when he ran into Scott, the master of U.S. colloquialism. Scott cut his teeth on popular slang, especially as a producer on the TV show, "Surfer Magazine." Alexei followed us around with pad and pencil and laughed with abandon, his head thrown back and his mouth wide open like a Muppet whenever he learned a new term. Hearing him say "dude" with his thick Russian accent was priceless. And, whenever Scott took the opportunity to teach Alexei a new word, out would come the note pad and, as he wrote, Alexei would repeat the word syllable by syllable as Scott would say it over and over, slowly. The look of glee on Alexei's face was a treasure when he was done writing and practicing the word and got Scott's definition. Scott loved being a source of education and amusement for Alexei. I loved how Scott was always so quick to laugh and find humor in even the smallest, most obscure event.

I'd love to share one of our fun experiences from Moscow. Perhaps this story says more about me than Scott:

Alexei invited us and some of his student friends to visit his family's small flat outside of town, which he shared with his mother, his sister and her small child. We were invited to high tea, and Alexei's mother served us a most incredible bounty.

The tea set was a complete, grand silver service which used the "pair of teapots" method of adding boiling water to a concentrated brew of the tea. Alexei's mother had prepared delicious dishes for us to eat. She was so excited to have Americans visiting in her home! This was a first for her and she was both nervous and excited.

This was one of the experiences in The Soviet Union when I was forced to confront all the images and propaganda my brain collected over the years since the years of Khrushchev. They were the enemy, after all. I was primed to think everyone was KGB. Of course, my Dad's cousin who worked in the State Department and was in Russia during the 60s told us they were KGB—probably even the young students we were hanging with. He should know, he'd interviewed Lee Harvey Oswald before he defected.

Well, KGB or not, here we were at this lovely tea. When Alexei approached me with a delicate china cup of tea and asked in his measured English, "Marcy, do you care about tea?" I answered (because we were helping him with his "American" and grammar), "Well, Alexei, I don't know if I care *about* tea, but I would care *for* some tea." His face went completely blank for a moment and then, when it sank in, he threw back his head in gales of that Muppet laughter.

After the other savory dishes had been served and happily consumed, it was time for the final sweet touch— blinis (blintzes). I was served a plate with a homemade blini, and Alexei held two shallow crystal bowls before me asking me to choose between the crème fraiche and berry preserves they contained. I said that I'd like both. He shook his head in horror and prompted me again to choose one. I repeated that I would like both. He said in halting English, "That ... is ... not ... done." I said, "I'm American and I would like to do it." (Wow, that was arrogant! I shudder at admitting this.) Much to his dismay, I dabbed some of the cream and some of the preserves on my blini and the room went stone cold silent. All eyes were on my first bite. When I put the fork in my mouth and made a yummy noise, it only took seconds before the young women in the room snapped back into their bodies and insisted on trying the combo. I can safely say I started a Russian revolution! Well, over blini toppings, anyway.

When it came time to leave the Soviet Union, the human rights group was less than happy with the outcome of their meetings. Scott and I, however, were completely high from the experience. New friends, a few words from another language that we repeat to this day (they come in handy with our Ukrainian neighbors), and forever memories. And we were closer and more in love than ever.

We had gained so much love and respect for Rabbi Shelly who led the group to the Soviet Union, that Scott and I asked him to officiate our wedding just over a year later. He was able to do a non-denominational wedding since neither of us is Jewish.

Between the years of our first date in 1987 and our 1989 wedding, Scott had proposed to me several times (at a stop light, in a couple different produce aisles, bombing down the freeway). But he would take back each proposal to let me know it didn't count. He had something planned and, when the time was right, he would do it. It had to be at a certain place and time. Mr. Romance personified.

Before any proposal could happen, however, there was the necessary "I love you" exchange.

That moment came when Scott and I were first together. We'd been together for a couple of months at least. Scott was staying over now a regular basis. It was a chilly night and we were cuddling in bed. I loved this time when we could hold each other close and talk and dream and feel our bodies molded together as one. I always loved that he loved to cuddle. Some men just don't, especially after making love, and it's such a lonely feeling when they roll over, out of touch. Done. Scott amazed me that he even seemed aware of me in his sleep. If I would get up in the night for some reason, as I'd come back to bed, he'd reach out and pull me in and wrap his arms around me as I fell back to sleep.

On this one night, out of the blue, Scott said, "I'm very hard to love." That was a strange phrase. What did it mean? Did this mean he was done; this was "it?" Was this the "we have too much of an age difference," or "I'm just not that into you," or whatever other kiss-off I could conjure up throughout the whole night as I lay awake? I couldn't ask what he meant because, you see, Scott said those ominous words just before falling fast asleep. "Hard to love?" I had to chew on those words until morning.

When Scott awoke, his first sight was me sitting up in bed, arms folded, and he knew something was wrong. Why wouldn't he? I'd sucked all the air out of the room. He asked me what was going on, why couldn't I sleep, and I reminded him where he had left off the night before. He was cornered. He sat on the edge of the bed and tried to shake the sleep from his foggy brain and speak. He couldn't get two words out before Mukti jumped up on him, put his paws on his thighs, and started licking his face with great gusto. It's important to mention that that was not normal Mukti behavior. He was not a kisser. And he certainly was not an energetic face-licker. Scott gently would place Mukti's feet back on the ground and start to say something else and it happened again. There was Mukti—literally in his face.

This happened several times until Scott looked at Mukti and said, "Okay, Buddy, I guess you have something you want me to say." He then turned to me and said, "So, without further ado … I love you."

What just happened? I thought this was going in the opposite direction. And I couldn't figure out how this amazing being could ever be hard to love. It was easy. All too easy. I had planned to stay single—at least for much longer. I was not proud of my string of failed marriages and knew, if I was going to take the plunge again, I had to get it right. I had to know what love is, had to be sure I knew what it means to be committed to someone. Little did I know the real meaning of "hard to love," and how that statement would be very significant later.

But I focused on the "I love you" part, and our relationship continued to flourish.

Before too long, that time came. No more stop lights, produce aisles and recanted proposals. The real thing came with a trip to the mountains, the perfect spot in nature as the sun was setting. We were there with Mukti, and the plan was to spend the night under the stars in the back of Scott's Ford pick-up. He had parked just so, and, as we sat and watched the sun start to set, its path was a descent between the two trunks of a majestic pine tree. And that's when he uttered the long-awaited words. This time, he didn't take it back. And I said, "Yes."

I loved our wedding. We did everything we wanted to do, defying themes and etiquette. After all, I'd had three before—big church in San Francisco, pool-side at my dad's house in Marin, backyard of future brother-in-law in Corvallis, Oregon. We had no one to please but ourselves this time.

We were married in an outdoor Unitarian Universalist amphitheater in San Diego's North County.

There was a big picnic area down a path from where we had the ceremony, and that's where we had the reception. The service contained a mix of quotes and traditions from several sources special to us. Yes, Rabbi Shelly officiated. There were nine best men because Scott couldn't single out one of them to be a best man. I had as many bridesmaids, my nephew, Kane, was our ring-bearer accompanied by my beautiful niece, Aynsley, who escorted our dog, Mukti, down the aisle to the stage. Mukti had to be there. He had that all-important role in our relationship for convincing Scott to tell me he loved me.

I wore an off-shoulder, white dress with a train, even though I'd be trailing it down dirt paths. So what? Not like I was planning to wear it again.

One of my maids of honor was asked why she had made the long trip for the occasion and she said, "Oh, I go to all of Marcy's weddings!" I have a slew of great, bright, funny, wise lady friends. You'll see.

And there it is. My dad gave me away for the fourth time. But this time, he also signed over the pink slip!

And our marriage began—April 29, 1989.

CHAPTER 9
BAIT AND SWITCH

It's hard for me to fathom how time has passed. Over 20 years of marriage? I know, everyone says time flies, there are songs and sayings and poems about it, but it is still somehow a shock.

Twenty years of being with the most thoughtful man; of creative birthday and Christmas presents which were always proof he knew me and my fondest wishes; of magical, elaborate, home-crafted Valentine's Day expressions of love; of plentiful, creative Easter baskets (in fact, two years in a row of home-made dark chocolate bunnies!); of our special Christmas Eve dinner with some of our dearest friends (a feast prepared by Scott unrivaled by any chef); and trips and walks and love and affection. Dear dog, cat, and birdie beings cycled through our lives and joined our happy household, as well as scores of possums and skunks and all manner of wildlife during my four years of wildlife rescue. We were both are animal lovers. Well, I guess that's obvious.

We stayed in San Diego for a few more years after we got married, but Scott had bigger dreams than San Diego production could fulfill. He wanted to make films and real

TV—write and direct in the big time. We'd often make the drive up to LA to pitch ideas to some of the networks, but it was as if there was a veil that separated the two counties. Though we could still get to LA within two hours if needed (about the same time it would take to get somewhere *within* LA!), it just felt like we would not be taken seriously unless we were in town.

We needed to be where the action was happening, so we bid San Diego farewell, moved to LA in 1996, and rented a home in North Hollywood.

Before long, we started making an acceptable living. Scott's best project during that time was writing and directing his own children's show which aired in syndication. A good friend was in distribution and had acquired a show called "Field Trip." He offered it to Scott to take over the project and rework it, and he proceeded to change the show completely. Yes, there were still field trips of sorts, but they were the result of two characters from another dimension who tumbled into the world of a young girl inventor, and they went on adventures across time and space. The aliens were Pug and Zero, and they were amazing puppets who stood about three feet high. Our partner in the show, Andy, was a good friend from San Diego who'd also made the move north to set up his special effects studio, and he designed Pug and Zero. He was also a puppeteer and brought in his good friend, Dave, also a great puppeteer. They were an amazing team, and brought Pug and Zero to life.

We hired friends wherever we could—our Editor and Production Manager from San Diego, and our Director of Photography was a good friend from Oakland. I worked on the rough edit and supported where I could in the overall logistics. The show was a playground of fun. There were challenges, of course, but they were far outweighed by the plusses. Kids and parents loved the show. We even had some of our out-takes air on Dick Clark's "Foul Ups, Bleeps and Blunders."

After a good two-year run, the show was cancelled. So, it was on to finding other projects. For Scott, that meant being brought in by a friend on a few reality shows—the genre was really taking off by then. He worked on "The Contender," a Mark Burnett show, as well as a couple of the grand finales of "The Apprentice." And there were others.

In 2003, I went to work for a non-profit organization, which had been my dream. It was a remote position, so I could work from home and have the best of both worlds. I loved the work and I loved being able to be at home with our dogs and the freedom to manage my own schedule. Though the pay was minimal, the job provided us with health insurance which would prove to be invaluable down the line.

That next year, after eight years of renting a house, we were able to buy our first home in the San Fernando Valley. That house was OK, but it was a tract house in a crowded neighborhood in the flattest part of the Valley. Just not my cup of tea. My heart longed for more of a country setting. I never was a city girl in the first place. Where I grew up in Fitchburg, it was very rural, with miles of rolling hills and woods. I enjoyed visiting cities, but could not picture living in one. And LA is the king of cities! A huge, sprawling metropolis with several large areas the size of any other city's downtown, all tied together with mile after mile of commercial and residential buildings, paved roads and sidewalks with just a smattering of trees and greenery. And the whole world knows about LA traffic. It's one of the worst cities for traffic anywhere.

We stayed in that house for a few years, but I was

warming up to making a case for leaving LA for ... well, some more bucolic destination. I wanted land and wild animals around me (not just the two-legged kind). After all, Scott hadn't quite cracked the "La-La Land" ceiling in his career, and I was starting to wonder if he ever would. Yes, things got better, pay got better, but he was still having to focus on work that would pay the bills, so he didn't have the luxury of developing new ideas or scripts of his own to feed the fire of his dream.

But my plea to leave wasn't necessary. The realtor who had shown us our first house told us about a house that was coming on the market in her own neighborhood in Woodland Hills, tucked up against the Santa Monica Mountain Conservancy. We agreed to go take a look at it that afternoon, and it was love at first sight! The house was perfect, right down to the upstairs and downstairs doggie doors. We had two dogs by then—our yellow Lab, Zuzu, and our Weimaraner/Rhodesian Ridgeback cross, Aria.

It was rustic—had the feel of a cozy cabin. The way it stood on the hillside, all you could see out the windows were trees, so we called it our treehouse, and there were windows everywhere. It was definitely in the country! You stepped out the door onto hiking trails in the Santa Monica Mountains. The sound of birds chirping and singing and crowing filled the air, and there were squirrels leaping from tree to tree with agility and glee. There was even an owl sitting on the telephone pole beside the house the day we went to look at it. Done! Where do we sign?

So we made the move to what was quite literally our dream house which we also nicknamed the "shut up, Marcy house."

That was 2007. We are still in our tree house to this day, and still in love with our home.

Over the years since we first moved to LA, Scott's

professional life still had its ups and downs. Work would come and go. We managed, but some years were tough for making ends meet. My non-profit job continued. Since it was remote, I was able to work from anywhere, including our new home.

Scott worked for various production companies when they had a project he was suited for, but the scales were clearly tipping in the direction of reality television. Though his dreams of being a writer and director did not go away, he took these projects to keep the home fires burning, and proceeded to move up the ladder to become a showrunner. He worked his way up the ranks through catfish noodling, shrimp fishing, gold mining and homesteading in Alaska. Don't even! I know, "catfish noodling!" Just look it up. You'll see what a sacrifice Scott was making producing some of those shows. His last, and most dramatic, high-production value show was "Dude, You're Screwed." I'll let that one sink in.

And that's why this chapter is titled "Bait and Switch"—because the man I married, wasn't.

CHAPTER 10
COULDN'T YOU JUST WANT A PORSCHE?

I really, really, really had no clue. None. Nada. Zilch. Zero. We have had friends now say, "Oh, that explains it," "I knew there was something about you, Scott," "you did seem like you were a bit guarded .... " But I didn't see it. I only saw my husband, My Love.

Now, lest you think I'm a ninny and that I've been painting an unrealistic view of a marriage, I will admit that it wasn't all roses all the time; we had our fights. I think that any two people living together are going to have their ways of doing things that are in conflict, whether it's a couple, family members or roommates. You either bury your issues or work them out.

I always believed in working them out. I believe in complete honesty. The only secrets allowed are around special holidays when gifts must be a secret until it's time to open them.

But we were talking about fights. Well, one of my favorites was when we were in a rollicking argument and I wanted to make a big, dramatic point, so I stomped out the back door on a freezing cold night, wearing only my pajamas. I made a big gesture of locking the door *before* slamming it behind me. Dramatic. However, it only meant I'd succeeded at locking myself *out!* I stood there in that cold realization when Scott opened the door and we both burst out laughing.

I don't like to fight. Remember, my parents did not teach us how. I like to keep my cool, until I can't. Oh, I can lose it! But I'd so much rather be Zen and cool and the calming influence. Doesn't happen as much as I'd like. And Scott was definitely his father's son: Loud, bombastic, big for the room.

And this brings me to what I need to say next; I can't put it off any longer. It's time to tell you what happened to us.

Fade in on a dark, early morning in Spring, 2008, the 19th year of our marriage. I smell coffee and see Scott standing by the bed with two steaming cups in his hands. This was not unusual except for the hour. We often shared a morning cup in bed, especially on weekends. And we always referred to it as "fawkey," the name my youngest brother gave to coffee when he was just a little boy.

When Scott sees I'm awake and sitting up, he bursts into tears, hands me my cup and says, "I don't know who I am."

This from one of *the* most confident people I've ever known. Was this the mid-life crisis thing? I couldn't fathom what might come next. Oh please don't ask for a Porsche or an open marriage or a separation … I was trembling. I tried to listen; I tried to be still and just be there.

Scott went on to say that he has "these feelings" every so often … feelings that he wanted to be a woman. He talked about how the feelings have "highjacked" him at times and he just gets caught in this reverie for hours or even days until it passes.

This just didn't make sense to me. It didn't fit. This was

the best *guy* I had ever known. He taught other women about the men in their lives and gave great advice. Our women friends begged him to "train" their own husbands and boyfriends to be more like him—affectionate, attentive, generous, romantic. He was loved by all his buds, he was his dad's "chip off the old block," his sisters' big brother and protector, his parents' only son, his mom's football hero. He was my hero, my man, my husband.

What was this? What did it mean? What did it mean to us? I was starting to think maybe a Porsche would be a welcome alternative, especially a bathtub classic.

We talked and talked. I asked questions; Scott tried to answer them.

He said he just couldn't hold in the feelings anymore without telling me. The words just blurted out of his mouth. He had to say something. He'd been awake for hours. In fact, he hadn't slept in a couple weeks.

There were no conclusions that day. There were tears and fears and questions and bumpy attempts at answers, but nothing definitive, nothing to hold on to. He even said he didn't think he'd have to act on these feelings but he just couldn't deny them anymore, fight them anymore, keep them from me anymore. For a long, long time, I hung on to his words about not having to act on the feelings.

I was numb. I knew nothing about this—I didn't see anything in my husband to hint that he might have feelings of being a woman, and I thought I knew nothing about the topic at all, though I started to recall some past experiences that told me I did know more than I first thought.

I remembered watching the movie, "Normal" in 2003, and being absolutely blown out of my shoes. I watched as the wife, played by Jessica Lange, moved into a place of acceptance and support of her husband, played by Tom Wilkinson, when he said he was a woman trapped in a man's body and wanted to live life whole, as the person *she* truly was. And I thought, No way! How could she stay? I could not see it; I didn't get it. I believe in love, but that's above and beyond.

And then there was that Oprah show when she had on the couple where the husband had transitioned and was living as the woman she always felt herself to be. I literally looked at the TV and said, "Well! At least I'll never have to deal with that!"

It wasn't much later that Scott came out to me.

A poignant and personal reminder of why I make it a practice to never say "never!"

Was this to be my life story now? No. Impossible. This was a phase, a mistake, a hormone imbalance. Scott was in his late forties, so any of those reasons were highly possible, right?

CHAPTER 11
CAN'T YOU JUST KEEP LIVING AS A MAN?

I just wanted life to go back to the way it was. I could not accept that any of this was real. It couldn't be happening, not to me; not to us!

Scott had lived forty plus years as a man, so why would anything have to change at this late date?

I would get lulled into a false sense of security when the subject wouldn't come up for a while. Maybe he just forgot, or it wasn't that big a deal and he was fine with going along as we had ….

But then I would ask and hear that there had been another highjacking. I would ask what it was like, what he felt, why did he think it was there. Scott would answer as best he could, but still sounded mired in his own confusion. His thoughts seemed scattered and his words were choppy. It was as if I were sitting in a small dinghy without oars being buffeted by the wind and the waves. Was he not sure, or was he not sure how to talk about it?

I have since learned that much of the hesitation and confusion for Scott was more about not wanting to freak me out with the information than it was a sign of his true feelings. He knew more than he was letting dribble out to me over time. He'd stop himself when he was starting an honest, frank answer because he would see the expression on my face. Guaranteed, I looked either panicked, angry, sad, scared, maybe even repulsed, so it was no surprise that he'd amend his answer.

Truly, my processing of this took me several years before I gained a clear understanding or any compassion for this. I'm telling you right now that I often felt I was going through hell and was afraid I would be banished there for good—destined to live alone or destined to stay in a relationship that was now damaged beyond repair, destined to never really know the whole truth. Hell had many scenarios.

I think it is important for you to know that it did take me years. I appreciate that people feel I am amazing and have handled something that they thought they would never be able to handle, but it was no walk in the park. It's probably the most difficult thing I've had to face. And later, you'll see that's saying something!

Scott and I did what any couple might come to. We talked about counseling. I thought we would go together, but Scott felt he needed to go to a gender identity specialist. He gave her six weeks to come up with an explanation of what was going on. A diagnosis, if you will. Of course, I hoped she would come up with something I wanted to hear.

It was literally years later when I understood that Scott already knew much more than he was telling me—he was quite aware of gender identity being the probable answer, and knew that he had been having these experiences and highjackings and desires to be a girl starting way back in early childhood.

I resented the gender therapist. I was jealous. I felt left out. I could only imagine what was being talked about "behind my back;" *decided* behind my back—without me, without my input, without treating this together, as a couple.

I felt deathly alone for the first time in many years. Where was I in all this? What was going to happen? What would this mean to me? What was I going to do? I was so completely lost. And I sure as hell couldn't tell anyone! At least not friends or family. What if this was a mirage and would blow over? I couldn't let this cat out of the bag if it was going to be put back in at some point.

I convinced myself that this therapist was not intent on helping people dig down and find out what was really going on and helping them through this weird phase of confusion, as I'd originally hoped. I felt she had an agenda, that she only wanted to help people transition, so I thought that she would just encourage Scott to go in that direction. I felt like this was driving a wedge between us, rather than helping *us* find a solution.

I was part of an us for so long, that was all I knew. I had received all I wanted. I loved the life we had designed, even when times were challenging. I loved our home and our animals and our language that was all our own. I loved our friends and celebrations. I had the job at the non-profit that I'd set my sights on for years. Of all things! How could this be happening?

Now I was walled out. What happened to telling each other everything? What happened to the husband who burst out crying one day early in our relationship because he just could not hold in how excited he was about a necklace he bought me? It was impossible for him to keep *that* secret. How could *this* have happened? How could he keep this big a secret? And how many more might there be?

Once you pull a supporting block out of the tower, the

whole tower can topple over. Remember that game? Except this time, I was not having fun with this game at all. It was my tower. I lived there.

What if the therapist told Scott he should start dressing and living as a woman? The what ifs just rocked me and drove me insane. My mind was so full of questions and images, and my feelings were a jumble of fear and betrayal. My world was falling apart.

I decided I needed my own safe house. I would find a counselor.

CHAPTER 12
JUNG UP TO DRY

Trust me, if Dr. Viscott were still alive, I would have run back to him in a flash. But he passed years before in 1996. I still think of him often.

Frankly, I'm not sure how I found the first counselor. Internet? Referral? Some directory. But I traipsed out to Pasadena and had the appointment. She was a lovely person. Didn't seem too shocked at my story, so that was a good beginning. And she proceeded to try to get to the root of *me*. OK, I'd worked for shrinks for years when I lived in Marin. I knew the drill. But I just did not have the patience to talk about me and who I was and what I wanted out of life and how I needed to start sketching and journaling. I just couldn't. I wanted answers—now. So, nice as she was, I didn't go back.

I found another woman sometime later. I think I chose women because I thought they would have empathy for my situation. Well, this second therapist seemed to. I liked her OK, too, but felt like she was too sympathetic with me, like she was taking my side against Scott. As much as I may have been looking for validation, I actually felt sorry for Scott in that room. Though I did blame him for throwing us, me, into this massive tailspin, my goal was not to sit around and commiserate. I needed answers. So, yet again, I didn't go back.

My next step was to do a bit more research. I'd always been a Jung girl, not a Freud girl. So, I thought a Jungian would be the best bet—someone who believed we all possess an anima and animus. How about that? Maybe it was just that Scott's feminine (anima) was coming through. After all, according to Jung, we all possess that combo. And, as men age, the testosterone declines and estrogen increases. This could be related to the shift in hormones, right?

I found a Jungian in the roster of therapists and gave him a call. He was warm and kind and willing to chat about this, even on the phone for a while. He seemed to understand the situation and gave me lots of reasons to think there might be hope and that this whatever-it-really-was might not have to proceed to the ends I was fearing.

We talked a couple times. I even booked an appointment with him for Scott and me. But that appointment came some months later.

CHAPTER 13
NANCY DREW

Fair warning, I'm going to continue to be very raw and painfully honest in this book. I think it's important for people to understand what this kind of situation can do to a spouse, or at least did to me. You need to know my arc to appreciate how I ended up where I did. I don't want anyone to think this was easy. It wasn't for me. Maybe others have a different experience. But the thing is, I had so far to go! Other people, given similar circumstances, may react differently. Things were already changing since I started going through this. But this is my story, my journey, my dark night of the soul and my reentry into the light. I am not going to sugar-coat.

The story continues ....

Scott was in the midst of the six weeks with his therapist. I would get dribs and drabs of information, but was not convinced he was sharing it all. And this just fed the whole case I was building about feeling left out and, okay, suspicious.

I felt like he was focusing on his life and leaving me out of the picture.

I just want you to know how wrought up I was about

all this, because I overshot the runway during this time in our lives.

Now, my elementary school friends will be the first to agree that I related personally with Nancy Drew. I loved the idea of being a detective like Nancy. When we playacted detective stories back then, I was often the one of our group who was given the role of Nancy. Of course, it was the early years of those great books and I had some of the earliest editions. Let's just say, when we were reading about Nancy Drew, she was driving a Roadster. 'Nough said!

So, I pulled on my virtual Nancy cap and decided it was time to do some investigating. If I couldn't be told the facts, I'd find them out on my own. I started with Scott's computer. Wow, for someone who said he could think like an outlaw, he sure left a trail to follow, starting with calendar entries.

Every week was an entry of "CW" at the same date and time. I figured out this was the therapist. I didn't know her name. I think if I had, I would have called to make an appointment myself. Oh, not to have her help me—to yell at her for taking my husband away!

And there was more! I'm not sure of the exact order of things as they occurred; they are a blurry jumble for me now. I think that's just as well. But all of what I'm about to tell you did happen.

CW wasn't the only calendar entry. On one date, I found this note, "getting better at walking in heels." *What?!*

This sounded to me like someone who was more interested in dressing like a woman than being content with the man he was.

Believe what you will about the importance of respecting privacy and not snooping in someone else's business. I didn't like doing it. I know this disturbed Scott when he found out. And, being Miss Honest, I couldn't *not* tell him at some point. But it took a while before I confessed.

This came down to being a matter of survival for me. I was desperate to make sense of what was happening. I needed more information in order to piece together the puzzle so I could see the picture. I didn't even have the corner pieces. I didn't have the picture on the box to go by, just distant, disturbing images of a couple being interviewed on Oprah and Tom Wilkinson in a dress. The one scene that haunted me for years from that movie was when Tom and Jessica Lange were sitting up in bed and it was the night before Gender Confirmating Surgery (GCS). Jessica says something like, "just one last time," and she lifts the covers to see the penis that was to be no more. I hadn't learned yet to never say "never!"

It's not as if I didn't try to find out more from Scott directly. I asked questions, and he answered within a comfort level he'd established for himself. But I just had this nagging feeling that there was more ... that I wasn't hearing it all. I was right.

He had gotten his "diagnosis" from the counselor after six weeks. He was told he was a "high-functioning transsexual." Now, I'm not sure I did hear that whole diagnosis. Scott may have put it to me that way. But I know he also chose words very carefully and would often leave out details that he thought might scare or worry me. Either way, the "high-functioning" is what I latched onto, because that meant he'd been able to manage all this time living his life as a man. That was encouraging to me because I thought that meant he could just continue. Why not? He was over 50. Who would want to change their whole life and identity at that point?

Truly, I couldn't understand why anyone would want to

be a woman anyway! It's not that great! Really! Right, ladies?

When I had the time, I would visit Scott's computer more. In a sub sub sub folder of documents (yes, this was an all-out invasion at this point), I found a document with a strange title. It was a story. A very graphic story of forbidden exploration and experimentation—of a woman kidnapped by another woman and commanded to put on women's clothes—written as fiction, a fantasy. But I had never heard language like that from Scott. He'd almost been modest when it came to sex talk or intimacy. He never seemed interested in porn, even if I suggested we both watch it. Even his bachelor party was tame. He told his tag team friends that he wanted a camping trip instead of strippers. Actually, he started a tradition that the rest of the tag team followed as they each prepared to enter into marriage.

So, when I read his story, I was shocked. This fantasy was bright red! Graphic details! Glaring! Who was this person? I didn't know him. I didn't know my husband. Everything I thought I knew was melting before my eyes and being replaced by someone who was downright raunchy in my mind; someone named Kendra.

During this time, Scott was very engrossed with the film he wrote and was directing, *"the kiss."* It's a vampire movie with a female Latina vampire as the lead, rescued by a teenage boy who falls in love with her. A love story, full of mythology and metaphor, love, sex and murder. As the lead vampire, Santa Maria says in one scene, "crazy, no?"

I was excited for Scott. This was a dream come true— to write and direct feature films was his career and creative goal in life. He was in his element. And I tried to help out whenever I could. That April, it premiered at the Lake Arrowhead Film Festival. It got great reviews, though it didn't catch on the way we'd hoped. With all that time devoted to the film, Scott had been out of the marketplace for some time. As we'd experienced in times before, our finances were really tight. The stress of that didn't help.

I was also quite busy that year with my work—at a shoot in early July out of town that kept me away from home through most of August.

Whenever Scott and I talked on the phone, I could pretend everything was fine. That was his voice, wasn't it? That was my husband. That was My Love. I was so desperate to have us fine again, whole again, together again. My love for him was so vast. I couldn't accept that there might be a flaw in the fabric of us.

There were these periods when things felt normal and I could go on about my work and life as if none of this had happened. And then, when my fears would take over, I felt as though pulling one thread of our fabric would unravel everything—unravel 20 years of marriage. A great and magical marriage. A marriage others envied and celebrated. The marriage I had always wished for. The marriage Scott would often tell me he had prayed for.

CHAPTER 14
HONESTY IS SUCH A LONELY WORD

Since Scott had cracked the door to me a bit, I wanted to step through into the room so we could stand in this together, work on this together, solve this together. Dare I say, "fix" this together. But, when we had our heart-to-hearts, confusion seemed to continue as the floor plan for our conversations.

I still thought (hoped) this was temporary; a mix-up, maybe a misinterpretation of feelings. So I suggested Scott go see the homeopath I'd been seeing for a couple of years. I knew a bit about homeopathy and how it works. I knew that many people will give homeopathic remedies, but it takes a good homeopath to know the exact remedy to prescribe. There are so many remedies, and several can appear to be meant for the same condition. It takes subtlety and a deep knowledge of the modality to hit the mark and choose the right remedy. And the remedies are not just meant for physical ailments; they work on all the sheaths of the body—physical, mental, spiritual, and the subtle body. If Scott's condition came from some interruption of energy in one of those bodies, I believed the right remedy would bring him back into balance. I even found descriptions of certain conditions in the homeopathic *Materia Medica* that supported my belief. Scott went to Jon and got a remedy. In retrospect, I do see that this was generous of him to do for me.

I would ask Scott how it was going, how he felt … constantly. I'm sure I drove him mad. And he would say he felt that the feelings ("highjackings") seemed to be pushed further back in his awareness, that they had less of a grip. Oh, how I loved hearing that!

There were times during that year that were so glorious, and there were also very dark times. It was such a rollercoaster. My emotions were tangled in knots—fear and dread of losing Scott in one minute juxtaposed with times of joy and love.

I did tell Scott about my fears: I would confess how I thought I could lose him; that he would want to leave me. After all, the cold feeling would wash over me that he was perhaps not the same person I thought he was. Whether this was something he was becoming or had always been, I didn't know, but that wasn't the point. What if I didn't fit in his life anymore?

His proclamations of love and forever were ardent and reassuring. He said he would always love me, had always loved me, and that would never change, could never change. He said he would not ever *ever* leave, and he knew that I loved him, too, and would also never leave. He was so sure! I wished I could feel as sure. But his words were reassuring. There were many times when the rollercoaster was taking us up to great heights and we were happy together on the ride.

When "*the kiss*" was happening, it was so much fun. And we could work together. I cherished those times. There were many nights and weekend days when we would sit and talk or just cuddle, and it felt as if things were "normal" (now there's an interesting word choice!).

We have a saying, "assuming the position." That is something we have done all these years: sitting on the couch lengthwise, Scott usually against the armrest, but sometimes we'd switch. The other person would lie up against the first and we would snuggle deliciously in our bobsled position. Scott would give me the most incredible head massages. It was like falling into a deep meditative state. Sometimes I'd fall asleep, but I hated to do that because it meant missing out on his magical touch. And we could sit like that for hours, watching TV or just enjoying the peaceful night.

But just as all rollercoasters go up, they also must come down. And though I reveled in the bright spots in our life, I didn't feel completely free. My mind would pull me back into the brambles of worry and the images of all I had discovered in my Nancy Drew investigations.

I started a secret journal where I could write all my thoughts and fears and questions—where I could scream at Scott or the Universe or God or whoever else I could blame. The place where I got stuck over and over again was around the subject of honesty.

I had had several relationships before this, as you may recall. I had had affairs and I had been with people who had affairs behind my back. I wanted to leave that kind of life completely behind me. No more! Honesty really is the best policy. I wanted honesty, honesty, honesty. Period. I strove to be honest about everything and had always assumed that Scott felt the same way and was always honest with me—completely. As I said, only holiday presents were exempt.

It's not as if I wanted to find out that Scott wasn't being honest with me. I would have been ecstatic to discover that he was! But I kept getting taken up short.

I always wondered if he had ever written anything in his journal. There it was—bedside table. It was full of beautiful descriptions of his spiritual experiences in meditation and meditation workshops. Beautiful, as best I could tell, because his handwriting is a challenge to decipher. He can write beautiful calligraphy. Let's just say, his journal was not written in calligraphy!

I could tell his last entry was a fervent prayer to God, but I couldn't make out the sentences. What I could read were the last words, "… wonder how I would live out my days." This struck me to the core. For the first time, compassion rose up in me. I saw how lost and consumed in despair one would have to be to say words like that. Final. Resigned. Unfulfilled. It made me sad. Did I want that for my husband; My Love?

This only emboldened my search for truth and understanding.

When I was looking in Scott's computer and found the entries I described earlier, there was one time when I also discovered some photos. When I saw them, I literally was not sure who they were of at first. I didn't recognize the woman in the pictures. And then … I did. It was Scott, made up and dressed up as a woman. Wig, high heels, short, tight skirt, the whole nine. I didn't recognize the location, and I had no idea who had taken them. "She" looked quite pretty. And I felt sick to my stomach.

Little Miss Honest here just could not take it anymore. I was hating my snooping and withholding of information as much as I hated Scott's concealment. And I felt like a total hypocrite. A hypocrite who was trying to survive and make sense of life, but a hypocrite none the less. So I told Scott I'd been snooping in his computer. I told him about the story I found and the calendar entry about walking in high heels and the photos.

He was furious. I had no right to invade his privacy, I'd betrayed his trust ... well, that felt very pot/kettle to me, but ....

Ultimately, he said that doing those things embarrassed him. He hated the photos and deleted them right in front of me. I was so crafty and so Nancy, I'd already copied them to a thumb drive. Why? Evidence or something? I don't know. I did end up deleting the drive sometime later.

Scott told me that the counselor had suggested that he should experiment with what it would feel like to actually put on women's clothes. She'd suggested he buy a bra, which he did, and he would wear it until he came home and then he would take it off in the car and hide it.

He found this other woman he went to for the pictures in some directory. She offers to support trans people by providing clothes and make-up and wigs and then taking photos of them.

All this was going on and I never knew a thing. Really, one of the things that bothered me most about this time, maybe as much or more than the idea that Scott wasn't being honest with me, was that he knew people, spent time with people, whom I'd never met. He was in a world that completely, and purposefully, excluded me. All I could think about was how I thought we had always done everything together—shared the same friends or at least knew of any that either of us had made when we were away from each other. But now Scott had secret friends, people who shared experiences with him that I had not—worse yet, that he felt he could not share with me.

Yes, Billy Joel, "honesty *is* such a lonely word."

CHAPTER 15
BUT WAIT, THERE'S MORE

In the summer of 2008, Scott left for a project out of town. I was home alone. Just me and our two beautiful dogs, Zuzu and Aria, who was two years younger than Zuzu. They were both so sweet and got along like close sisters. Aria would often curl up directly on top of Zuzu, who would be curled up, asleep on the couch. We called that "stacking dogs." They were great company for each other and they were great comfort to me when I was home alone.

Scott was to be away on his project for many weeks—a perfect time for Nancy Drew to return.

Part of my investigation included visiting the web. Not a great idea, may I say. I was trying to get educated about transsexual, transgender, whatever the right heading would be. Oh, trust me, there is information on the web, not all of it very helpful. Ever looked up a disease you were concerned you'd contracted or were diagnosed with? Then you know! Sometimes you can get too much information.

I was extra sensitive to that because I'd learned my first TMI lesson at a young age. When I was given a school assignment to write a paper about what my father did for a living (suddenly sounds sexist, now that I think about it), I went to my mother and asked her the question.

She looked at me in disbelief and said, "Why don't you ask your father?"

I replied, "I don't want to know that much about it." That has stuck as a family saying ever since.

The thing is, I knew that my dad knew almost everything, and this isn't to say he *thought* he knew everything, he *did* know almost everything! That could be helpful to a curious child much of the time. However, with homework deadlines, it also meant that a simple math question could lead to an explanation of how computers run on zeroes and ones. Sigh. Great, but I just wanted to know how to solve a word problem that started with, "If Sally is knitting a sweater while riding on a train from Boston to Bangor .... "

The internet was way worse than asking my Dad! You *can* find *everything* there and some of it is frightening! There were all sorts of descriptions and graphic explanations and personal experiences and horror stories. I mostly wanted to get a sense of what happened to relationships when one of the partners transitioned. The subject was addressed by lots of people and, as I'd start to read, I'd think, "Ah ha! Great, this sounds like something I can relate to." Not! The story might start out innocently enough, but it unfailingly took a turn and went down a road I had never traveled and didn't want to.

But, here's the thing: as much as the information may have been disturbing to me at the time, at least the subject wasn't so new anymore, not such an unknown world. Just by visiting these sites and reading about what transgender is and all the various ways people and their partners and families were dealing with it, whether or not I could relate to it, the veil lifted a bit. I was peeking in and feeling a little less ignorant. I think that gradually led to my being a speck more comfortable with the subject. Fear was morphing into curiosity and a desire to learn more.

Some of that curiosity also led to wanting to know more (OK, everything!) about Scott's situation in particular. And an opportunity presented itself.

I was going over our cell phone bill and trying to figure out why the charges were so high. I reviewed our call history as well as our data. I noticed a phone number in Scott's list of calls that I did not recognize. As I checked further, I saw that it appeared very often. I also noticed that there was a call to this number stamped in the wee hours of one morning: 2 a.m. That seemed strange. It was also right after a call he made to me. Our call lasted a couple minutes, this other one lasted many minutes more. Who was getting more air time than I was?

So, once Scott was home again, I looked in his phone when I had a chance and found the number. It was assigned to a woman's first name. There were also other names I found as I scrolled on the recent call list, and I didn't recognize a lot of them. Some seemed in code even—initials or a single letter. I tried the number, but there was no voicemail message, so I didn't get an idea of who this was.

During these weeks and months, though Scott and I were talking about things a bit more—by phone while he was away and also once he came home—I was still getting truncated answers from him, explanations tossed over his shoulder, made light of. Why? What wasn't he telling me? I may not have gotten the full picture yet, but I do take credit for having a healthy intuition and psychic ability. So, I couldn't let this go. I kept wanting to be wrong, but I kept finding things.

I told Scott about the mysterious phone bill and asked about that number. Now I felt more like an inquisitor than a detective, but I wanted to get details from Scott, not from snooping anymore.

This was a bit of a shift for me because I wasn't trying to steer, wasn't focusing only on my desired results and denying the possibility of where this could lead. Maybe knowing the truth, knowing everything, would somehow help me understand better what Scott was going through, understand better what this meant to the two of us. Maybe it would even bring us together again? Maybe having knowledge would be more powerful than living in questions and the pain of not knowing. Maybe I could handle the truth.

Scott was willing to tell me about the mystery phone number. This is someone he met who was going through similar circumstances—feeling he was really a woman in a man's body. They related to each other, they talked about what it was like and what they were doing about it. He also admitted that he went to this person's house "once" where they dressed in women's clothing that the person kept at his house, and went out. There were a few bars around town that were safe for them.

This person was married, and his wife accepted this about her husband. I could not fathom this. But it did kind of fascinate me that a woman, a wife, could reconcile this in her relationship and … stay. I turned this over and over in my mind. I wondered what it took—how does someone get there? How does someone make it OK, make it work in their marriage?

And Scott explained that he just needed to experiment—to figure out how deep his feelings went, how real they were. He needed to try it on for size.

I was grateful that he could share some of this with me. Maybe he was feeling safer and more open, and maybe I was, too. But, as much as I felt there might be an opening in our communication, something would inevitably happen that would draw me back into feeling that I didn't know the whole story.

And sure enough, there it was. I was cleaning our closet and found some unfamiliar women's clothes tucked away in the back of a drawer Scott must have assumed I would never find.

Wow! And I couldn't believe his taste in clothes, BTW! Really? Not my style at all. Were we even so separate in *this*?! Yeesh! The clothes were kinda slutty in my book. I had left miniskirts back in the '60s with my bell bottom pants and Famolare shoes. I was always avoiding high heels. They were painful! I could never get the hang of walking in them. But my "husband" was going for it.

This pushed me back a step in my progress of being willing to look at the truth, and of feeling Scott was being completely honest with me. Did I have to step into my Nancy Drew role again to find out what wasn't being said? Well, yes.

I used a reverse directory to find an address to go with that one repeated number in Scott's phone. Late one night, I drove to that part of town and saw the house with that address. I snuck down back alleys and through some back yards to get closer, hoping I could see in the windows. Trespassing? What had become of me? Come on, admit it, there is a certain air of excitement that comes with sneaking around. Adrenalin on high alert, all senses tuned to the task at hand. My heart was racing. In a way, I was discovering a new part of me—the lioness who would do anything to protect her pride (perfect word, eh?!). I liked it just a little. I liked the sense of danger and intrigue. I was living this, not watching a show on TV, or imagining that Nancy Drew had this quickened heartbeat and shallow breath as she searched a hidden staircase in an old mansion.

I tried to get closer to the house, but couldn't see in the windows. And then, some guy came out on the porch and turned on the light. It felt like a spotlight!

I mumbled something about being lost and quick-stepped my way out of there. I went back to my parked car (of course a couple blocks away. What self-respecting detective wouldn't think to do that?). And I drove home, all cells on fire.

It wasn't long after that that I confessed this location scouting to Scott. I think he was a bit more shocked than mad. He was worried for my safety and my sanity, I think.

And I think this created a shift in him. He got a taste of how deeply all this was affecting me and how very desperate and isolated I felt.

Though up until this point, he had not been interested in seeing a therapist together, he was now amenable. He accepted that we might need outside help after all, that this was bigger than both of us. Since we were starting to share more, I just didn't want to make any mistakes that might set us back. I felt we needed a third party to walk us through these thorny subjects and feelings. I was concerned that, since feelings were still strong and on the surface, we would have difficulties expressing ourselves without leaking hurt and anger. He agreed, and even agreed to see the Jungian therapist I'd spoken with on the phone months earlier.

I thought this guy would help me express what I was going through as well as maybe present to Scott the animus/anima theory to explain what he might be going through. Yes, OK! I was still hoping to be "right" about my diagnosis. Yes, I can hang on when something feels like a life and death scenario.

At first, the session wasn't bad. The therapist seemed to listen to both of us and be fair to both of us until he turned to me with some rather harsh statements which took me off guard. His tone was accusatory as he stabbed me with his piercing gaze and told me I was being selfish and unfair. Why couldn't Scott live his life as he saw fit? Why was I trying to control him and block him from being his true self? My face was burning hot. I felt shaken as well as betrayed, since I thought this therapist was going to be more "on my side." Scott rose to my defense and told him not to speak to me that way. I was singed by the fire of the therapist's words and grateful for my hero coming to my rescue.

Wow, could it be that My Love, even if he was changing, was not changing completely? Maybe I wasn't losing the person I had loved so much all these years.

The last straw was when the therapist told me, "Maybe you just have to get in touch with your inner lesbian." We'll just let that one land for a moment. Take it in. Breathe deep. Maybe you feel it was a wise and accurate thing to say. At the time, it blew my circuits. It blew Scott's, too. Scott was so livid because he recalled my experience around that word at boarding school, and knew it was a rough time for me. We left and didn't return.

I still think about that line in disbelief, but I must admit that my reaction to it has been taking a turn, and my disbelief has been morphing into thinking it might be valuable advice. Maybe there is a way to get in touch with my "inner lesbian."

Scott and I had always approached our life together with the belief that we could solve any issue ourselves; together. But this one was quite the lollapalooza, so help seemed like a wise choice. But with this last therapist and the ones we'd seen individually, it just seemed that nobody got "us." In the same way that I could not relate to the individuals I read about on the internet who were going through this experience, we saw how there was something quite different about us—our life, our love, our marriage. Some women were fine with their husbands dressing in women's clothing. They thought it was fun. Some people were not tied to a rigid view of sexuality. Maybe they were Bi; maybe they had an open marriage where they could have other sex partners. These were things that did not fit in our world. We loved each other deeply, we were committed to being monogamous and to keeping that love alive.

We went back to talking about working on things ourselves.

CHAPTER 16
HEALTHUS INTERRUPTUS

The rollercoaster was still alive and well. With starting to talk and share and be more open, we were healing a lot of the pain. Throughout all the ups and downs, we always had the thread between our hearts. There was never a doubt that we loved each other. In fact, it's because our love was so strong, so primal, that I had the depth of fear and pain that I did. I didn't want to lose what we had. This love mattered to me! This marriage mattered to me. I was determined from the beginning to be in it forever.

At this stage, I confess I did still hold out for Scott's feelings to continue to be pushed to the far recesses of his thoughts. I hoped the experimenting would help convince him that this was not for him and he would return to being the husband he always had been. And, again, when he was away on a production (happening more and more at this stage), I could lull myself into that safe zone. I could talk to him on the phone and be with My Love the way we always had been. Sometimes I would ask how he was (the loaded question), but we would often avoid putting toes in that pool and would talk about our days and how we missed each other.

It was during one of these times that I decided I didn't want my journal anymore. I didn't like that I was maintaining my own secret, even if it was meant to help me let off steam and get a grip. But it felt as if having the journal was almost an affirmation of Scott's other side (what to call it?). So, one night, I lit a fire in our fireplace, ripped out the pages and burned them a few at a time. I glanced at the writings one last time as I placed the pages in the flames. I meant for this to be a ritual to purify the whole scenario as well as my darker thoughts. I later found I was far from done.

Just when I thought I had the full picture of what was happening with Scott, he shared more about his relationship with his friend. He told me they had gone out to bars several times, not once, as he first confessed. His friend also wanted to fully transition to being a woman, GCS surgery and all. Scott said this was something he would never want to do. Oh, and news flash, the friend's wife was leaving him, uh, her.

Gradually, the bar of what he wanted kept getting moved further and further out. Now he was saying that maybe he would want to go out once in a while, dressed as a woman. That might assuage the feelings when they came up. Now *there* was a big test for me. I still bristled at the idea of him doing things without me, and yet, I could not fathom the idea of doing this *with* him. How could I reconcile all this? How could I support My Love? How could I keep my love? How could I fight him when he was sad about how he would "live out [his] days?"

But all those questions—his and mine were soon to take a back seat.

Over a year had passed, now. It was the summer of 2009 and I was out of town again for a month on a work project. On July 14th, I was doing some exercise in my hotel room. I had been doing sit-ups and stopped to rest after a few reps. I lay my hands on my abdomen and I felt as if there were a slight mound under one of my hands. If I raised my head to look, I couldn't see anything, my abdomen was flat. But when I lay back down, it still felt like there was something there that didn't belong. I became concerned that it might mean I had a cyst or something. So, I decided to have it looked at at a local clinic. They did an ultrasound and said there was, in fact, a mass on my ovary. In fact, I had a smaller mass on the other ovary as well. They could not tell from the scan what it was; whether it was malignant or not. I had no symptoms and felt fine, so I decided to check it out when I got home.

A month later, Scott and I were in the office of an OB/GYN at my HMO, Kaiser Permanente. She saw the ultrasounds, did an exam and suggested I go in for a biopsy.

I am not a fan of "Western Medicine" in general. I'd rather take herbs than drugs. I'd rather put myself in the hands of my homeopath and Ayurvedic doctor than someone in a white coat. But this doctor wrote two columns on a piece of paper to show us the pros and cons of acting and not acting on this. The cons were pretty dismal.

So, after a very high CA-125 blood test result (over 1,000 when under 35 is the normal range), and some other tests, I was assigned to another OB/GYN and an oncologist. The plan was to send me in for a laparoscopy and they'd be able to biopsy the tissue. He and another surgeon would perform the procedure.

Remember my reference to the word "never" earlier? Well, this added to collapsing a whole new string of nevers! I was *never* going to need "Western Medicine" because I had such good alternative care. I was never going to have surgery. I was never going to get cancer (though my mother died of breast cancer at 56)....

With the possible surgery factor looming on the horizon, I felt it was important to get a second opinion, and a friend gave me the name of her doctor at UCLA Medical Center.

When I called the office for an appointment, I found he was going to be on vacation for two weeks and would not be able to see me until after that. Well, that would be too late in light of the date range I was given for surgery. Rats!

But later that day, his nurse called back and told me he could see me the next Monday! In fact, I spoke with him on the phone right then for a few minutes. I said this was weird because he was to be my second opinion but I'd be seeing him before the appointment with my doctor to discuss what my treatment should be. He laughed and said it was fine to have the second opinion first! So, I grabbed the appointment.

He was terrific. He explained a lot about ovarian cancer, since this seemed a likelihood, and he gave me an exam, including an ultrasound.

He said he did see masses and that, if my doctors wanted to go through with surgery, even a hysterectomy, he would agree with that approach. He also clinched the deal by asking who my surgeons would be and, when I told him, he said I had the best in the biz. That reassured me a lot.

A couple of days later, my OB/GYN called to confirm the UCLA doctor's "second opinion" that I should have the laparoscopy and that I'd get a call soon to let me know what that date would be. He said I would first come in for the pre-op when we would discuss all the options and the procedure in detail, and that it would probably be in about two weeks. This was on a Wednesday.

Two days later, I got a call saying there'd been an opening in the surgical schedule the following Monday and that I could come in for the pre-op the next day, Saturday. So much for the two week window! But I rather liked that I had no time to get anxious.

I had never had surgery before; never been anesthetized. I admit that I was a little excited about the experience of being "put under." There had only been three times in my life when I came close to having anesthesia. The first was when I was ten and was to have my tonsils out. All my friends had talked about what it was like to be put under, and it sounded like fun. Of course, *my* ear/nose/throat doctor had to be the exception. He wanted to use a new procedure where I would only get shots of Novocain in the back of my throat and he would remove my tonsils while I was awake and sitting up in a chair. Oh, my God! I can recall the torture as if it were yesterday. One of the worse parts was the sound of the scalpel as he cut away at the back of my throat. He was also brusque enough that my mother was horrified and told him to take it easy. After all that, I discovered that everything they tell you is BS. I didn't even *want* ice cream my throat was so sore. And I'd been looking forward to that treat the whole time.

My second time to *almost* be put under was when I was about 22 and was scheduled for periodontal work. The periodontist told me that I'd have laughing gas. I had heard great things about what it's like when you have Nitrous Oxide, so I was looking forward to the experience! We were well into the procedure when it seemed to me I'd only had Novocain and no laughing gas and tried to ask the doctor about it while I had all sorts of dental instruments sticking out of my mouth. He said he didn't give me laughing gas because I seemed so relaxed already. I told him that I was relaxed *because* I thought I was getting laughing gas!

Then there was the time I had a (benign) lump removed from my breast. Local anesthesia, and the procedure was done right in the doctor's office. That was an experience all its own! The surgeon's nurse had had so much plastic surgery, she looked like one of those creepy characters right out of the Twilight Zone! And, when the doctor asked for a certain size suture, she brought the wrong one. I offered to go get it (as I lay there with an open incision) because I knew a bit about medical procedures from my wildlife rehab experience. I guess I was quite chatty through the whole procedure. I asked if all his patients talked this much and he said, "Marcy, my patients don't usually talk at all!"

Now, here I was with my fourth chance at being put to sleep. I doubted they would resort to Novocain this time!

The laparoscopy was scheduled for Monday, September 14th. During the pre-op meeting with my OB/GYN on the prior Saturday, he had explained what they were going to do—start with laparoscopy for the biopsy and go from there. If the biopsy showed positive for cancer, there could be several additional stages in the process, including the possibility of a full hysterectomy. After he walked me through what could happen, he had me sign a bunch of paperwork. One sheet was my agreement that, if I did have a hysterectomy, I agreed to not have children. I looked at him in complete bewilderment—my RCA dog head tilt. He said, "I know, I know. Just sign it." I asked if that meant we were ruling out the possibility of immaculate conception. Got a smile out of him on that one, and he said we'd cross that bridge if we got to it. Wow! The ways hospitals have to cover their butts these days! At 61, I wasn't exactly planning to get pregnant anyway.

Early Monday found me on a rolling hospital bed in the surgical ward, getting prepped—gorgeous gown and socks and cap. My legs were wrapped in a warmy, massagy device to help my circulation. Now *that* was something I would have liked to take home.

Scott was by my side.

The anesthesiologist, Dr. Sha-naa, arrived to explain what was going to happen and give me a little something to relax me. I asked if he was going to have me count backwards or sing his name (you have to know music from the 50's to get this), and he laughed. I said that I was blown away that I'd gotten to this point and hadn't asked any questions. I didn't even know what questions to ask. I didn't even know what drug he'd be giving me!

He said, "Michael Jackson drugs."

I said, "Eeeeeek!, I don't know if you should tell people that. It didn't work out so well for Michael."

He said, "Ah yes, but I know how to administer them!"

I was happy to have someone with a sense of humor knocking me out.

Then I got the relaxing shot and they started to wheel me away. I was sinking fast and giddily waved over my shoulder to Scott, saying in a totally blotto voice, "Bye bye My Love!"

So, yes, ovarian cancer, complete hysterectomy. Not what I wanted or expected. But there it was—the long zipper on my abdomen, held together with staples. And this is *modern* medicine?! And chemotherapy to come. It took a long time to sink in. Scott was so loving and supportive. Cooked for me, made sure I was comfortable and pampered at every turn. He knew how hard it was for me to give myself over to this "Western" approach in the first place. His Lola Granola wife could not rely on herbs and homeopathy and acupuncture and Reiki at this stage.

The surgery was September 14th. On October 9th, as I was recuperating at home, walking up our road a few paces and back a couple times a day, I got a call from my Dad's hospice nurse up north in Novato. She said Dad only had about 24 hours. So, Scott and I packed, got in the car, I put a pillow over my belly under the seatbelt, and we drove the six hours to the Bay Area. The pillow was mostly for protection from the rubbing of the seatbelt. But at times, I felt like it was there to hold me together.

We visited my Dad the next morning and he was out of it. I whispered prayers and mantras into his ear, and then my youngest brother came with his two daughters just before our father took his last breath. My oldest brother was not able to make it. Frankly, he was incarcerated. But he did call, and I was able to put the phone to Dad's ear so Macky could say goodbye. My second oldest brother, Morgan, got on a plane from Texas and called when he landed at the San Francisco airport. We put him on the phone to Dad, too, because it was looking like he wouldn't arrive in time to see Dad in person. Dad faintly smiled after each call and took his last breath within two minutes of the second call.

Needless to say, the events of the next months pretty much shoved the whole thing with Scott to the back of the closet. (How could I resist a double entendre?)

So, home to chemo treatments every month for six months, balding, and several more nevers now crossed off my list.

CHAPTER 17
THE MADDEN HATTER

I'm not going to go into a whole blow by blow about this period—monthly chemo treatments and graphic details. But I do want to share some stories from this time. They'll tell you a bit more about me, and I also hope they reassure some people who are freaked out about the "C word" and how I approached this chapter in my life.

We hear over and over about the importance of positive thinking. It is important to be positive, but that's a pretty broad topic.

First step was, luckily, that I kept my sense of humor! Survival experts will tell you that's the first sense to go when you're in a tight spot.

I was raised in a house of humor. Being punny (spelling intentional) was par for the course. My mother was like a cross between Phyllis Diller and Lucille Ball, except in looks. Mummy was beautiful. My dad was a wit himself. Sharp and bright. And, by the way, he was also a looker! My school friends thought he looked like Sean Connery and swooned over him. He didn't mind a bit.

Humor is definitely in our blood. My brothers and I are a pain to be around because the jokes and puns fly constantly.

It's not that cancer was funny, but there were endless opportunities to find humor all around, including being able to joke around with doctors and nurses and other patients in the chemo ward. After all, this wasn't a picnic for any of them.

Even in a life and death situation, you can choose what to put your focus on, and I chose to focus on life. I knew death was going to come one way or the other, but I didn't have to encourage it by being down, or being depressing to others.

I also took into account the language I was using. Words are extremely powerful in affecting our state and determining our outcomes. Just Google "As a Man Thinketh" and see what you get!

I concentrated on using uplifting words, and I chose to change some words altogether. For example, since I believe in offering service to the planet in some way, I renamed "cancer" "can serve," because I wanted to be able to live and continue to serve the world in some way. Instead of "chemotherapy," I named my treatments "kemosabe" because I thought of the medication as my partner, my side-kick, in healing. I'd share this with other patients in the chemo ward, and they loved it! They could see the value in treating chemotherapy as a friend rather than a poison.

A dear friend had encouraged me to repeat a mantra when I was getting chemo. I pictured the medicine entering my body *as* the mantra and clearing out the unwanted cells. I asked the chemo to focus on those cells and promised that I would focus on protecting my healthy cells.

Visitors would come and go—bringing gifts and love and foot massages and smiles and sweet encouragement. My heart was filled with gratitude. I was so fortunate. There were angels all around me and Scott was at the head of the line—always there when he could be.

I had six rounds, three weeks apart. After round two, the hair was getting thin. I had it cut off and donated, and our dear hairdresser came to the house to shave the rest. Ironic. I had thought about what it would be to have a shaved head years before. Monks would do it as a sign of detachment and letting go of karma. I figured I could never be a monk; I could *never* shave my head. There's that "n" word again!

When I started chemo, the hospital handed me a huge stack of paperwork, and much of it was about the side effects I could experience from chemo. I took the stack and immediately handed it to Scott, asking him to read it.

I said, "If you see me exhibiting any of these symptoms, let me know. Otherwise, I don't want to know what they might be."

That was another way to protect my thoughts. I didn't want to be jumping on every little itch or tingle and think it might be a side-effect. I was concerned I'd create conditions when they weren't really there.
I've since learned that that's a real thing—something the medical community now acknowledges. It's called the "nocebo effect." For some patients, the mere suggestion of side effects is enough to bring on negative symptoms. Interesting, eh? Glad I had heeded that direction from Dr. Viscott years before to trust my intuition.

I did well during those months and did not have much at all in the way of side-effects. Day three after each treatment was the toughest. I felt nauseous and very weak and tired. But my dear friend, Eleanor, was a miracle worker with her delicious chicken soup.

I had to exert a great amount of effort to stay afloat in a positive attitude. Ovarian cancer has a bad reputation for the lifespan factor, and not everyone knew how to talk to me.

I had to apply the "Thumper Rule." Remember from Bambi? The rabbit, Thumper, was known for saying, "If you can't say something nice, don't say nuthin' at all."

I asked people to only speak in a positive way. You'd think that would be easy! I remember one man starting to tell me, "Oh, my sister-in-law had ... " and I stopped him. I recited the Thumper Rule, and he said, "Oh no, this is OK. My sister-in-law had ovarian cancer, but she died of it." Well, *that* was uplifting! If that's being positive, I never want to experience your negativity, Buddy.

And then there was the well-meaning friend of the family who sent me a get-well card. When you open it, it played back Gilda Radner's voice doing her Rosanna Rosanna Danna character saying something about getting well. I can't remember that part because I threw the card away in horror. Hello?! Gilda Radner died of ovarian cancer. Now, this person didn't know that, and I know she was being thoughtful. But it was a big ouch at the time. Ew!

And then there's the advice. Reams and heaps and piles and emails and website links and personal experience of remedies and supplements and special cleanses and diets and gemstones and incantations and ... it was quickly getting overwhelming.

My solution was to ask questions, do research and start to pick and choose the things that resonated for me—a supplement from here, a remedy from there until, after a while, I felt I had landed on what I could handle and what seemed like the best form of treatment for *me*. After that, I closed shop and my ears. When people had more suggestions, I'd explain that I had what I wanted and was content, and I asked them not to make more recommendations. Yes, I did include Cannabis oil. I found a reputable grower who would make the oils and ship them to me. The CBD oil was OK. I would put some drops in an empty capsule and take it that way. However, the Cooperative I was working with also encouraged me to take some THC, saying I'd get more healing benefit from elements of the whole plant. Whoa! First night, a dose of THC the size of a sesame seed. I seemed to tolerate that fine. So, next night, I went with a dose the size of a grain of rice. When I reported back the results, my contact at the Cooperative said I was sensitive. I'll say!

I sat on our couch and did not even dare to move my eyeballs! Scott said I gave him flashbacks to his high school dates. Oh, I was not a happy camper! I had done my share of drinking in the past, but had escaped the pot-smoking world. Though I did live with a dealer in my 20s.

There I was on the couch all these years later. I felt so zoned that I knew if I moved one muscle, I was done for. I sat as still as I could. I said I needed to go to the bathroom and Scott said he'd help me. No! You don't understand, I could not have *crawled* in there! I had to stay frozen or something terrible would happen. Well, then came the nausea and the reason for Scott's high school recall. Pots and pans and trash cans cycled before me as I surrendered the contents of my stomach. If this was anything like the high people went for when they smoked weed (OK, I'm old. Insert your own hip name for it here), I just did not get it. I could not wait for the room to stop spinning and to stop feeling like my body was under siege.

Over time, I got a bit better at the dose size and also built up some tolerance. But there were still those times when I miscalculated and spent a good couple hours lying on the cool tile of the bathroom floor.

Scott teased me relentlessly! Now maybe I'd like Cheech and Chong movies ... no! Never! But I do have to admit that, after all those years of avoiding using cannabis for pleasure, here I was taking it as a medicine. What was becoming of me? Again, I ask, how many nevers was I going to have to face? Well, here is one never I can stand by--*never* say "never!" Because, guess what ... never never ends.

Though I dreaded one particular side effect of chemo most of all, it turned out that being bald was not so bad. I got so many compliments for my "perfect head," and how would I have known that if it were still covered with hair? The feeling was freeing. I liked going for walks on our nearby trails and feeling the breeze and the sun on my head. It made me feel new.

And I collected hats! I just did not feel drawn to wearing wigs. People gave me hats and made me hats. I was surrounded by generous beings. At treatment time, dear friends would drop by. Scott had arranged with a couple of our dearest friends to drive up from San Diego to stay over ... bringing delicious food, some of which was prepared by another friend who wasn't available to make the trip but sent along amazing, healthy dishes. Cat would come with sacks of food and spend a night or two. We would talk and talk. She is a wise and brilliant woman and every conversation is a deep exploration into the heart and soul of us and of every topic we cover. And there are many!

Debra was my Matron of Honor those twenty-something years before. She, too, would drive up and stay with me, give me amazing craniosacral treatments and we also had warm, rich, healing conversations.

Our dear friend, Jill is an oncology nurse with a nearby hospital. She would come see me in the treatment room and bring such light and love and fun gifts! Since she knew a lot about cancer and treatments, she was also a wealth of information. The best gift of all were her foot rubs. Oh, I highly recommend them!

We are blessed with such dear, generous, loving, healing friends!

Whenever Scott was home, he was there to swaddle me, hold me, massage my smooth scalp and shower me with love. My love and appreciation for him grew by leaps and bounds during this time. A lesser person would have reacted quite differently. And in our case, Scott was putting his life questions on hold again in order to help me through everything.

January 29, 2010 was my last chemo treatment. My markers were normal and I could get back to living. I had taken time off work to recover from the surgery, but I had been able to continue working throughout the kemosabe. Luckily I worked from home, so I didn't have a commute or have to worry about how my hat looked that day, unless we had a Skype meeting, that is. Even then, I only had to be concerned about how I looked from the waist up. PJ bottoms and warm slippers were neatly hidden from sight under my desk.

It may seem that I glazed over the death of my father earlier. It happened exactly halfway between my surgery and first chemo treatment. Losing him was a big landmark in my life, and it meant that now both my parents were dead. My mother died way too early, many years before. My dad remarried, and his second wife died too after they had been married 25 years. Dad was 93 when he passed. He had lived a good and long life, and his passing was not a surprise. But he was such a huge, influential figure throughout my whole life that I would never stop missing him. In fact, I wish I had stayed longer to hear his answers to my questions, rather than feeling I didn't "want to know that much about it." I feel him with me to this day; my mother, too.

I was grateful to my parents for all they had imparted

to me—their wisdom, their strength, their will to live and their humor. And it was now time for me to focus on my health and life.

During the course of my kemosabe, I wrote this:

May we all know and remember
the power we have
to change this world for the better.
May we experience
that our hearts are brimming over with love.
May we remember our Source
with gratitude and bowed heads.
May we take solace in each other's company
as we walk this path together.

2010 was a year of healing. I had regular follow-up appointments with the Oncologist and OB/GYN, and I was seeing an Ayurvedic doctor who had me on a program of herbs and eating and avoiding certain foods.

My hair was growing back. I was feeling stronger, able to exercise more and adapt to eating even healthier foods. Jeez, there wasn't THAT much to give up. I ate quite healthily to begin with (usually), but there is always room for improvement.

That summer, I went to my work's headquarters again and was so well received. People were happy to see me healthy. I suspect, they were happy to see me alive.

CHAPTER 18
HOOK, LINE, AND FOOT IN MOUTH

Life was a big distraction for both of us over the next months. We were trying to get back on our feet. I was very dedicated to my work and health, and Scott was doing what he could to rustle up some work. We were both pretty good at "acting as if."

Every once in a while, I'd ask Scott how he was doing. As you know, I was really asking, "How are the hijackings?" "Are they gone?" "Can we go back to being who we were, now?" His answers continued to be just vague enough, and delivered in just the right amount of reassuring words that I could relax. That is until I would get the now all too familiar waves of fear wash over me and I would wonder if this was really behind us.

Then there were the times Scott would admit to having the feelings well up, and he was just not convinced that he was born in the right body.

Since I was healthier now, we returned to the life we had put on hold when I needed to focus on getting well.

We returned to the life of one step forward, two steps back. Nothing was truly resolved. Questions did not really have viable answers. There were some doozy screaming matches. The anger, sadness and fear I had shelved for all those months came crashing back! Truly, I'd faced a life-threatening disease and was trying to deal with that, work through that, get past that, and now I had to be here? Be in this situation? I make a concerted effort in my life to not ask "why me?" I think it's just as important a rule as avoiding the never word. Somehow, I feel like it's, as my brothers used to say to me all the time when we were little, "cruisin' for a bruisin'!" However, I have been known to say out loud, "really?!" Is this really happening? There are just times when it is hard to believe the hand that just got dealt.

I've heard that trying to control what happens in your life when things are challenging is like gripping the armrest of your seat as your plane is about to crash. I felt like that so often—afraid and maybe facing a big crash.

That's why those times when life felt almost back to "normal" were so precious. I clung to them with all my might and with the hope that they would last.

We lived inside this yoyo for some time. Status quo and then status woe!

At least in 2011, the work potential for Scott started to turn back around. He had capitalized on his previous reality TV show experience to land a job that summer about catfish—"Hillbilly Handfishin.'" He was sent to the Red River in Oklahoma to shoot a series about noodlers—them folks that stick their hand or foot in an underwater crevice or hole in the rocks lookin' to get bit by a giant catfish. Yep! A real sport, and there were some professional characters who did it down there for a livin.'

The premise of the show was to take real city slickers down there to OK, stick 'em in the river with the professional noodlers and try to bait a catfish. Literally! Cuz they were the bait!

The production company cast the most obvious fish out of water (how could I resist?) types that they could— models, business folk from the city … you name it. You know, city slickers.

I visited Scott for one long weekend there. I don't know how he and the cast did it! Hours and hours every day in that river! It's called "red" for a reason. Eeeeeek! And you could not see $1/100^{th}$ of an inch below the surface. So, you'd be wading or swimming in this, not knowing what was there—and it was much more than catfish, I'll tell you! Deadly cottonmouth snakes that can swim well, and gar fish that would leap out of the water if they saw something shiny. Too bad one young blond bombshell cast member didn't pay attention when she was told not to wear jewelry and was smacked in the face with a flying gar angling for her earrings.

I know how to vacation, right? But I wanted to be with Scott, and this was a way to steal some time together. At times like this, we didn't have to "talk," you know, about "it." I could tag along on the shoots; we could go on walks at night (careful not to step on a rattler or scorpion. LOVE Oklahoma!), and I could see him in his Producer role. Somehow, that reassured me. He had to be a strong captain. He was the man in charge. Seeing him like this was familiar and comfortable to me. His voice would get so strong and confident when he would bark out direction to the crew. He handled the high-maintenance "talent" and the guest cast with great diplomacy as well as strength. He could solve the issues in a way that everyone felt heard. Well, almost everyone.

That job ended for Scott before the time he'd been contracted for was up. There had been a conspiracy among some of the crew and "talent" who reported negative stories back to the production company. Scott's phone calls with the production company got weirder and more toxic. It turned out, the wife of one of the hosts was the one who targeted Scott because she thought he was the one who was standing in her way of being on camera. She wanted her 15 minutes and then some! Ironically, Scott had been her champion and was her one and only supporter for having any screen time. If anything, her husband didn't appreciate her sharing the stage. And the crew weren't fans of hers either. But she attacked to Scott like a giant catfish, and insisted he was the culprit and had to go. Scott was fired.

This was hard on both of us because Scott took great pride in his work, and I was quite attached to the idea of a regular paycheck! Now what? Where would the next job come from? We were expecting the project to last for weeks more—through post production supervision. Now Scott was back to looking for work.

There was one upside to the whole fiasco. Scott did make a life-long connection with a Comanche Chief who "adopted" him as a son, and gave him a blanket and a private ceremony to bless him and protect him from ill-doers. Who would you rather have watching your back?

Scott came home, but luckily it wasn't long before another project came up. The unfortunate part was that would take him out of town again.

We used to say we would never be apart for more than two weeks at a time. That promise had been long gone by now and would only get stretched more and more. Weeks were now becoming months and I was home alone a lot.

Over the next few years, certain things started to happen.

CHAPTER 19
SCAVENGER HAUNT

Catfish "noodling" was only the beginning of a long string of reality shows that took Scott away from home and into the far corners of the world.

After Oklahoma, Scott was only home for a few weeks and then another Reality Producer job came up and he went to New Orleans for shrimp fishing. Now that was a sad state of affairs because it was after the BP oil leak fiasco. That unfortunate event took a huge toll on the people of Louisiana, and especially the fishermen.

When Scott wasn't out on one of the boats in the fleet, he would be acutely aware of the Halliburton presence everywhere—a huge compound near his hotel and black helicopters flying overhead on one mission or another. A whole story all its own.

In September 2011, I joined Scott for a long weekend in New Orleans and we had a great time together. It was those romantic get-aways that gave us some time to breathe and just "be" together. Amazing what a change of scenery can do. We had a lovely room in an old New Orleans hotel.

There's something about staying in a hotel that is exciting to me. When I was a child, whenever we traveled and stayed in a nice hotel in New York or Boston, for example, I got so giddy. The reverberating sounds of doors opening and closing down the hallways, the elevator transporting people to and from their destinations, the fresh linens and towels, and furniture and surroundings that were all new to me. I'd sit in my parents' room and watch them get ready to go out ... during those times, I felt like a princess in a fairy tale.

Having times like this with Scott had that same effect on me. It felt special, and now I was the grown-up getting ready to go out for the evening. Magical! We talked and walked and ate—boy did we eat! One of our favorite memories to this day was eating at John Besh's "August" restaurant. Scott wanted to find a restaurant for the show that used local shrimp in their menu, rather than having them shipped in from outside the country. I had done some web surfing on my own for Scott, found August and the menu, and suggested it. Well, because they knew there might be a TV shoot there and that Scott was the Producer of the show, they pulled out all the stops for us! Though we did order from the menu, we kept receiving surprise dishes "from the kitchen." I would have to say that night was the best dinner out we had ever had! And we got a tour of the kitchens as well. Kitchens, plural, because one kitchen was for preparing the main dishes and there was a kitchen on the second floor just for pastries and desserts. On our way back from dinner, we strolled through the French Quarter. It was buzzing with tourists and locals and students on break and clubs and street bands on many a corner. There were old hotels with balconies overhanging the street and architecture that can only be ascribed to New Orleans.

That was the same night I ended up singing "Proud Mary" with a curbside quartet. They invited me over and I went! It was fun to flex that muscle again and not let shyness get in the way. There was something in me that wanted *and needed (?)* to just break out and be a bit crazy. I love to sing, but many people would probably prefer I kept it to the shower. I did the usual choir and glee club stuff in school and got into folk in my teens and 20s. I had a guitar and could hold my own at a party. But ever since my mother had told me, "You can't carry a tune in a paper bag," I had a complex about singing. Let that be a lesson, parents! Please be careful what you say to your kids. Some words stick forever.

New Orleans was like a cool oasis in my life which was otherwise in an upheaval.

Okay, now on to what I said about "certain things started to happen ..."

From 2011 through 2014, Scott was traveling a lot. More reality shows were to come after catfish and shrimp. And there were times I was traveling for work, too. Sometimes, I'd be home while he was away and vice versa.

I remember one day when I was home that I got in our Toyota Matrix to run an errand. This was more Scott's car than mine. I have a 1999 Celica convertible that I love! But there are times when the Matrix is better when I have a bunch of stuff to buy or Goodwill bags to drop off, etc.

As I reached down to shift into gear, something on the floor caught my eye. When I picked it up and examined it more closely, I saw that it was a broken fingernail—one of those Lee Press-On nails. Well, it for damn sure wasn't mine! As part of my health watch, I avoided any chemicals that might get into my system and compromise my health like hair dyes, nail polish and commercial shampoos. I was just a *little* sensitive about all that, as you can imagine. There was only one logical answer to where this broken nail came from. And it made me go cold inside.

Then there was the time not long after that when I was watering our potted plants on the patio. As the water filled one of the large pots that held my purple potato bush, I saw something white float to the surface. What? A cigarette butt! With lipstick on it. I don't smoke, Scott doesn't smoke, and no one has smoked at our house ever— certainly not inside the house or our yard, and our yard is completely fenced in. It's not as if a passer-by might have dropped the butt in there. And last I looked, our gardener, Miguel, did not smoke or wear lipstick. So, as much as I hated to admit it, there was only one conclusion.

I finally brought myself to ask Scott about these things. If I wanted him to be honest with me, I felt I needed to be in full disclosure mode myself. And Scott did admit to the artificial nails and the cigarette. There was some evasion and hemming, but, to his credit, he did fess up. He said he'd dressed a couple times ... just had to try it at home. But smoking? That blew my mind. Scott said something about a young girl has to experiment with these things. As foreign as that sounded to me, it was one of the first times I became aware of the disconnect; that there was a difference between the Scott I thought I knew, and this other identity inside him. How could Scott not smoke but still want to when this alter ego was calling the shots? What *was* this? Was it like having multiple personalities? That's something I had dealt with a long time ago.

When I worked for psychiatrists in the early 70s, I got a call one day for one of the doctors. The woman on the other line was rude and abrupt and insisted on being put through to the doctor. It was the office policy that I not do this when the doctor was seeing a patient in the office. But this patient got so abusive and belligerent on the phone that I did buzz in to the doctor and apologized for interrupting before explaining the situation. He said it was all right and to put her through. After a short time, I saw the light in the button on the phone go out, so I knew they had hung up. Moments later, the phone rang again. It was the same woman, but she was very soft spoken and her voice was warm. She apologized for the earlier call, explaining that "she" had taken her over and made the call to the doctor, and she was so sorry that *she* had been so rude to me. I told her it was fine, and that it would be great if this second personality would be the one to make the calls from now on. After I hung up, I had qualms that I might have set that patient back years by saying that to her! I talked to Dr. Lamers about it and he gave his Santa Claus jolly laugh and said it was fine.

Could this be the explanation for Scott's behavior— Multiple Personality Disorder?

This *next* incident is one I had blotted out until I started writing this book. It's appropriate that I tell this here because this is part of a string of experiences that helped me start to turn my ship in the choppy waters that had become my life.

Dr. Lamers had a couple scheduled to come in one day. They were both very attractive. Classic good looks on the man—could have been a GQ model. The woman was exotic and beautiful. She had long, black wavy hair and a figure that was like a real-life Barbie (who would not topple over!). She was the epitome of femininity. After being in the waiting room for a while where I was able to chat with them a bit, the doctor came out of his office and invited the two of them in.

After the hour's appointment, the couple left and Dr. Lamers asked me if I noticed anything interesting about the couple. I knew he was driving at something but I clearly did not know what, so I shrugged and said I didn't. With a smile on his face, he explained that the woman was a man.

Now, again, this was in the early 70's when proper terminology about transsexuals or transgender people was nowhere near part of the mainstream. Even the medical and psychological professions were struggling with how to name this kind of phenomenon.

When I typed up the doctor's notes, I discovered that the reason the couple had come was because of the man's feelings. He was questioning his own sexuality; he was afraid that he was gay because, even though he had fallen for this beautiful woman, she was "really" a man. She had male genitalia. Wow! At the time, I thought the whole thing was fascinating, and I thought it was too bad that the man was having such doubts and fears about himself. Anyone who had seen the woman he was with would have agreed that she was a beauty, and no one would have guessed she was anything other than a woman.

See? Isn't it interesting that I had this whole experience back in my early 20's and had somehow stored it way in my subconscious. A message?

In fact, there's another experience from the past that came flooding back in to my consciousness with all this, and it was something I could not figure out at the time. Now I have a better understanding of what the symbology was.

Journey back with me to 1992. Scott and I were on a TV shoot in India for two weeks.

Being in India is like taking all the volume and color saturation knobs on your viewing and listening devices and turning them up to the max. The colors are intensely vibrant and can burn your eyeballs, the sounds are a strange symphony of familiar and unfamiliar noises, and the smells … ah, the smells. Smoke mixed with fragrant flowers, some not so fragrant elements, incense, and teeming life.

We visited temples and teachers and mountain shrines

and, during the annual magh mela, we took a boat out onto the water at sunset at the sacred confluence of the three rivers, the Ganges, the Yamuna and the Saraswati where hundreds of people were wading and dipping in the water to be cleansed and to pray. I took the opportunity to pray, too. The energy was thick with the vibration of something other-worldly; something hallowed.

Since Scott and I were into yoga, we felt deeply affected by being in the land where yoga was born. We were so grateful, even giddy to be there. Though the host of the show was far from home, including mentally and emotionally, Scott and I felt very much at home. We were curious to see and try everything. Despite the challenges of a small crew with lots of equipment to lug around, and despite the show host's mini tantrums, we thrived. The crew were all good friends of ours, family really. We were all like kids in a new playground.

One day, we visited a Jain temple near our hotel in Mt. Abu. The temple was built into a hillside and had no decoration or indication on the outside that it was a temple. This was to protect it from attack at wartime. It just looked like part of the rocky hillside, disguised so it could not be seen from the air.

Once we stepped inside, we were in a wonderland of carved marble. It took the craftsmen years and years to complete the work. There was room after room of intricately-carved marble and every inch of space was done—floors, ceilings, walls and columns. Often, there were carvings within carvings—one carved marble column within another. It was as if the whole temple was made of the most delicate white lace. In some places, you could look into an anteroom and see other shapes and figures that were so tucked away it seemed we weren't even supposed to see them. One such room had two huge, life-size marble elephants! I could just see them through a lacy wall and door that was only cracked open.

And there were statues of deities and saints surrounding the outer circle of the temple. They all had brightly-painted eyes that, when you stared at them, drew you into a deep and meditative state. There was one such statue that completely had me mesmerized. I just had to keep staring into those all-knowing eyes. I was filled with a feeling of warm love. I felt completely connected; completely one with that being and with everything around me. And Scott was there, too, seemingly in the same state. When we compared our experiences, Scott told me that, as his gaze was locked on the statue, he saw himself reach back to the middle of his shoulders, grasp a zipper and unzip from there and up over the top of his head, until the sheath that was his body just fell away, revealing a body made purely of light. As the sheath fell away like a lightweight Halloween costume, he stepped out of his skin to stand as the new, light being, who said to him, "I'll miss Scott. He was really fun." I was confused by that and a bit frightened. It sounded as if Scott was not long for this world! Was he going to die? Scott didn't seem very concerned about it, so I didn't say anything about the questions it brought up in me. He seemed deeply touched by the experience. It was amazing.

Over the years since that trip to India, I would flash back on Scott's experience in the Jain Temple, and I often wondered if he did, too, if he relived the words, "I'll miss Scott. He was really fun."

Now I know each of us did revisit that experience many times. And now those words have a different significance to me. I had taken the experience then as a spiritual experience where Scott was becoming less attached to the physical world and identifying more with his Universal Self.

Yes, he was less attached to the physical, but not necessarily for spiritual reasons. This was real, physical, a direct hotline to who he was. He was less attached to his body because he never felt he belonged in it. He probably felt like unzipping it and stepping out of it most of the time, and yet he might have to stay encased in that ill-fitting costume for the rest of his life.

The experience in the Jain temple shook him, and yet he could not talk to me about what it truly meant to him; how it scared and freed him all at the same time.

Now, as I was trying to reconcile the whole idea of Scott dressing and smoking and wearing fake nails, I was looking for signs to help me understand him more. I even wondered how our dogs were responding to him like that—looking and being so different! I mean, after all, of course they wouldn't recognize him or, dare I say, approve! I mustered the courage to ask Scott. He told me that the dogs were fine. They accepted him no problem, played in the yard as always and gave him our favorite puppy kisses.

You may find this strange, but that was one of the things that helped me. If Aria and Zuzu accepted this, why couldn't I? What did they see or know that I didn't? Why weren't they afraid or suspicious of this stranger? What were they tuned in to when Scott looked nothing like his usual self?

This was a crack in the doorway that let just the slightest sliver of light through. The light that would gradually flood in and take over my whole way of looking at what was happening. But that was still a ways down the road.

At this point, my mind and heart were a house divided. I couldn't believe Scott was dressing at home, and I couldn't imagine how that looked, though I tried. And I'd see-saw between wanting to know, wanting to see, wanting it all out in the open and feeling like I could never do that, never see that, never reconcile that "side" of Scott.

I did still hang on to the thought that Scott was "confused" about who he was. After all, those were the first words he uttered to me that fateful, early fawkey morning years earlier.

It had been the belief that he was just confused led me to make an appointment with the Jungian psychiatrist. But, you know that story. When the doctor said to me, "Maybe you just have to get in touch with your inner lesbian," that closed that door shut. My circuits fried and I felt my face burning hot with embarrassment and feeling betrayed; exposed. When Scott jumped in and said, "Don't speak to my wife that way!" He was there to my rescue. My protector. With all the changes in our lives we were facing, I got to see that some things are consistent; some things are reliable. He still was my hero. There was a familiarity and comfort in that.

I was waking up to the fact that Scott was making many concessions for me. I was drawn to wanting to do better by him. I had been very caught up in my own fears and anger, and had not been very compassionate about what Scott was going through. I had seen his actions as something that would hurt me; would damage us and our marriage. I hadn't thought much about his pain and his own fears and all that he had been doing for me—to make me feel OK, feel secure; to support me as I went through cancer and the treatments and the side-effects. He had put his life on hold time and time again.

CHAPTER 20
COLOR ME ORANGE

Was there some way I could be more open about all this? Scott had grown his hair pretty long. That was fine, I liked it long. And then he announced that he wanted pierced ears. Oh my.

With both long hair and even earrings, he would still be well within the box marked, "male," at least in LA! So, I rallied with an "OK" and went with him to get his ears pierced. It felt like participating in some of these things would take the sting out of the division that was created by Scott doing things without me. It was getting to the point where that was bothering me more. I said before how important honesty was to me. Maybe by peeling back the layers that had built up as protection, I could feel connected to him again. I had allowed myself to be wrapped in caution; waiting for the proverbial other shoe.

I admit I was hoping that giving in on these compromises might mean we had reached a finish line. In other words, maybe with long hair and earrings, Scott would be content. In fact, he had even told me that then. But I later learned that he was saying that for my sake.

One of the consolations of his traveling so much was

that I got to choose my own TV shows to watch. I had heard a lot about "Orange is the New Black," so I started to get into it—guilty pleasures for the Marcy-at-home scenario.

And here we are again at that place where little message grenades are strewn all around. Really? A transgender character in the show? No one had bothered to mention that. But damn if I didn't like the show! And, actually, watching the story of the transgender character, there was a small part of me that was glad to be seeing it, glad to have a peek into that world from a safe distance.

But yikes! There was the scene when Laverne Cox, playing Sophia, was dressing for the first time at home where *her* wife could see her. When the wife came in, she got over what was obviously shock and sadness, and helped her "husband" put on one of her own dresses. It was too small, of course, but gave enough of an idea of what Sophia could look like in nice clothes. Then she agreed to do Sophia's make-up. She tried to make a deal that she would do that if Sophia would keep her penis. No deal, but the wife helped Sophia put on make-up anyway.

Here I was, talking to the television again, "I could NEVER do that!" I could NEVER help Scott put on make-up! How did she do it? How *could* she do it? Why? How could she be party to turning her husband into a woman?

In the long run, I think the show helped me in some ways. Just by virtue of exposure alone, I was getting a bit more familiar with what transgender is and what it's like for the person who is in that situation. I saw the drive in Laverne Cox's character to be the woman she knew she was, and to jeopardize everything to get it—even her marriage and family. Laverne is trans herself, so that added an element of authenticity to her portrayal.

But the most significant thing about that show is that it existed in the first place! Here I was, watching TV as my little escape from the world, my world, and look what happened! There was nowhere for me to hide from this. There were rumblings about Bruce Jenner being trans!

CHAPTER 21
THE WISDOM OF JESSE JAMES

I turned to meditation and contemplation to find strength and meaning. I needed to tap back into my deep-down trust that everything is perfect, though appearances can be deceiving and I can get caught up in the illusion!

I also turned to the wisdom of Scott's father, Jim. Scott had shared a saying of his dad's with me, and it started to become my mantra: "You can go strapped across the saddle or sitting up in it, but you're going ridin', Jesse James!"

Wise man, Jim Madden. Yep, it was starting to be pretty clear that I was on this road, this journey, this ride called life. And, as part of this life, there were various destinations I was supposed to visit. I could not dismount until it was my time. But I could choose *how* I made my way along this road. I could be tall in the saddle, confident that I was heading in the right direction, or I could be draped like a victim over the horse's back, out of control, not even able to see the scenery along the way. I chose to sit up in the saddle. I *choose* to sit up in the saddle. This is still an important guide for me and has stood me in good stead through these years.

Believe me, the road keeps unfurling before us and our horse is still destined to carry us down it. I was far from "done" with any of this—any of this journey with Scott, any of this journey called "life" and what it presents us. We never know what might be around the corner.

As we moved into 2012, work for Scott kept getting better. At least he was moving up the ladder of producer credits. But "Bamazon" was a pile of poo. Gold mining in the Amazon? Run by a country boy from Alabama? What could possibly go wrong?! The surroundings presented their own challenge—thick jungle to plow through, insects the size of B-52s, the most poisonous snakes in existence. And T.E. the "star" and client of the show was a pile of problems.

Again, Scott was gone for months—January through July—first on the Amazon and then post production in New York.

The shoot turned out to be a bear. Though Scott had laid down strict rules about no boats on the river at night, T.E. wanted to get back to camp, even though darkness had already fallen while he was on a location shoot with a cameraman and the Executive Producer, Scott's boss, Monica, a trusted professional, and great friend for years. Despite her protests, T.E. insisted they pile in the boat and head back to camp.

Two accidents on the river that night! Monica was thrown from the boat and could hear the alligators scatter when she hit the water! She easily might have drowned if the cameraman hadn't gone fishing for her. She was desperately flailing for the surface not realizing that she was so disoriented, she was swimming toward the bottom of the river. So, back in the boat, they headed out again, all admonishing the boat driver for still going too fast. Sure enough, the boat hit a tree trunk that was hidden just under the river's surface, and everyone was thrown into the bow of the boat. Monica had the camera in her lap and was thrown against the seat in front of her.

Eventually, they made it back to camp. Someone woke up Scott and he jumped into action, getting updated on what happened and having the nurse assess Monica's injuries. She said she couldn't help Monica and that there were probably broken bones and internal injuries. Once Scott found out that the whole risk document had been mocked up by T.E. to just pass the insurance requirements of the production company, Scott had to improvise and he sprang into action. He rallied some of the troops for help and started making call after call on the satellite phone.

Early next morning, Monica was on a "heli" to Venezuela. She's a warrior. After basic treatment and a short respite, she insisted on going back to the shoot and then on to New York for post. Scott's and her time in NYC was cut short, however. They were pulled out of finishing the edit of the show. By then, Monica had a better idea of her injuries and was looking to the production company to assume responsibility. She ended up having several surgeries on her shoulder—major, major injuries, and law suits. A pure nightmare.

Scott came home that spring and had interviews for two more reality shows. One was on repo-ing vehicles in the south, and the other was about gathering survival experts from a variety of disciplines and sending them to a remote part of the world to see how they survived.

The money on the repo show was a bit better than the other. However, the SKYPE interview with the producers of that show started with asking Scott, "How do you do with difficult people?" That's all I needed to hear. As Scott was happily saying how well he does with challenging people, I walked around in front of where he sat on the couch with his laptop and I pulled my top up to flash him to shock him out of the delusion. With catfish and shrimp and gold mining, there had been a greater than normal dose of difficult people already!

The survival show sounded like it had real possibilities. And the people in that production company had a good reputation and came across as very professional.

As Scott, weighed the pros and cons of the two shows, I sat down beside him and put my hand on his knee. I said, "I have done my best to stay out of your business decisions when it comes to picking shows to work on and negotiating your fee, etc., but this time, I just have to say, 'no to repo!'" I then said, "I want my husband to work on a show I can be proud to tell other people about!"

We laughed and laughed and Scott gave in to my request. Happily, a higher rate was also negotiated for the survival show, so Scott didn't lose any money in the process.

The down side was that the production company wanted Scott in Denver. Summer and fall of 2012, Scott was gone. I was alone at home again, left to my "Orange is the New Black" and other forays into the world of transgender. And Bruce Jenner was more in the headlines, sporting a ponytail amid speculation that he had had plastic surgery.

I did my share of further research on the web. Now I was looking more for the medical, technical discussions, looking to understand what this was. I still had a hard time reading the shares of spouses and of the trans people themselves, though I did hang in there in order to get more understanding from everywhere I could.

CHAPTER 22
WHO DO YOU TRUST?

One of the toughest things I faced was not being able to talk to anyone. Now, I grant you, this was self-imposed. We have wonderful, caring, spiritual, deep friendships with a few people, and I was chafing at the bit to talk to one or more of them.

I say not talking about this to anyone was self-imposed because I think, subconsciously, I thought that speaking it would make it real. What if it was a phase after all? Then the cat would be out of the bag and we could never get it back in!

But one day, I was walking with my best friend, Leslie, and the words just came out: "Scott feels that he is really a woman."

What she said then surprised me. She took it almost in stride. The idea was not shocking or repugnant to her. She talked about the world being full of diversity and that there are many variations of sexual preferences and gender identities. I was so surprised at her perspective and how open she was to the whole concept. I had thought it might be a deal-breaker in our friendship—*What?* Your husband thinks he's a woman?! But, instead, she ended up making me feel better. If my friend could be OK with this, why couldn't I?

But I still felt strange talking about this to anyone—to talk to anyone without Scott knowing—or being OK with telling this friend. I didn't bring it up again and I kind of hoped she'd just forget about the conversation.

I had other friends I longed to talk to, not just because we are close and I don't like having secrets—especially one as big as this!—but because I also felt I could use more help. I seek the input of friends on many issues in life, and it felt strange to dance around this in our conversations.

I could always speak about Scott in glowing terms: how well he was doing on the show, how much I missed him, how entertaining some of his stories were.

Sometimes, he would go for a long walk at night in Denver and call me then. So I went on his walk with him by phone as he downloaded his day, talked about the production company staff, and all the logistics they needed to handle for this gargantuan show. They were planning some very obscure locations to shoot in, ones that would present real physical challenges to the talent—five survival experts from various disciplines. Of course, that means the crew is also up against all the challenges and dangers that Mother Nature has to offer "out there!"

Oh, and did I tell you the name of the show yet? "Dude You're Screwed." Yes, I know. You're catching on to this synchronicity thing and how funny life can be, right?

So, "Dude …" was well on its way. 2013 saw the production of season one. Scott was in his element. He was busy and happy and traveling all over the world. This was his thing. He got to be just creative enough to satisfy his appetite. Even though what he really wanted to do was direct. And write. And, well, a few other things! But this was a good solution for the time being.

But then, the other shoe literally did drop.

CHAPTER 23
HERE WE GO AGAIN

The year had been going along pretty well. My work was good, and we had a regular check coming in for Scott's work again. I relished paying bills and putting some money in a savings account.

Of course, I also had plenty of time to mull over our life and situation and wonder where it would all end up. There were still so many questions! Was Scott going to go for it and come out as a woman? Did this mean dressing like a woman all the time? Make-up? What about hormones? Surgery? As much as I wondered about Scott, I wondered about me. If this was going to happen—any or all of it—what was I going to do?

I did wonder about leaving. I pictured what that would look like. And every time I did, I just saw how entwined our lives had become. We were ... we. I wasn't afraid to be alone, that wasn't it. But by now, after all these years, Scott and I were a package deal. We loved each other. We had our language. We could recount an event or a joke by using just a key word. We had crazy nicknames for our doggies. We had rhythms, patterns, traditions and shared memories. Our friends envied what we had. They knew how close we were and they could feel our love. It was tangible to them. My women friends were very vocal about wanting "a Scott" of their own—or at least for Scott to train a guy for them. He was so thoughtful and affectionate and loving. He was a great cook and conversationalist and he lived life so enthusiastically. My friends wanted that. When I thought about leaving, I just could not visualize where I would go! What would I be leaving? Whom would I be leaving? Don't forget, I had already had more than my share of marriages before Scott came along. I did know how rare it is to find someone to love, who loves you, and with whom you are compatible enough to live together for years…happily!

Maybe I was leaning more toward staying, but I also felt trapped, resentful. Why had he married me if he had all these other feelings going on the whole time? I would have been free to live my life because I was quite sure that, if he had told me anything about his feelings when we were first together, I don't think I would have stayed with him. I was not interested in being with a woman, thank you. I would still have looked for my Prince Charming. Did he know that? Was that why he had kept it all bottled up and hidden for all those years? Well, among other reasons, yes.

But, hey! Lest my life trot along with only this much tension and angst, I got to fall down yet another rabbit hole. It was time to put things on hold again to deal with a new health intrusion.

It was an evening in August, 2013. We've gotten personal enough by now, right? I could just not go to the bathroom. You know, "number two." The urge was intense, but as much as I sat and tried, I had zero luck. Funny, when we were little and wanted to tell Mummy we had to go potty, we would say, "I have to try." For years, I thought "try" was another word for "poop." Anyway, nada. I could not "try."

So, yet again, it was Elena to the rescue. She drove me to the Kaiser ER where we spent hours with all sorts of fun tortures. I mean ... holy shit! Only not really. There were pills and enemas (yes, plural!) and nothing, and she helped me with all of it. Now that's a friend! I opted to go home to see if something would work after a while because nothing had yet. No. Still no luck. So, Elena took me back when I called to say I had painful cramping and still no luck.

Back at the hospital, it was more of the same attempts to clear the dam, and then some tests. I still remember lying in the bed in the ER cubicle and waking up to see Elena's head on the bed by my side. She was sitting in a chair with her head on the bed and had fallen fast asleep. I tear up every time I think of that. I think about how good a friend she is, how devoted and dedicated and unselfish and loving. I have made it quite clear to her that when my time comes, I want her and her partner, Laurel, to be there with me. There could be no greater spiritual cheerleaders to help me cross over than those two angels!

So, this is how the night had passed, and it was now about 4:00 a.m. A tall, dark, all business doctor walks into my postage stamp sized area, puts his hand on my knee and introduces himself as the surgeon on duty. He laid it all out for me—what I was now facing. His eyes were dark and piercing, and riveted on mine. He clearly wanted my full attention. And, without losing his laser grip on my eyes, he continued to speak.

He told me I had a blockage of my intestines—on the descending colon. He called it a tumor. He said that it meant my cancer was back (I don't like calling it "my" cancer. That feels like I have too much attachment to it and that it belongs to me. Not a great approach when it's something I don't want around at all). It had been four years since my first diagnosis.

The surgeon said I would require colostomy surgery.

They would go in, remove what they could of the tumor and the affected colon area, pull part of my intestine through a hole in the abdominal wall and create a loop called a "stoma" which would reroute the stool. I would need to wear a bag that would hang off my abdomen from now on. You can figure out the purpose.

He continued to stare at me with his arrow eyes and asked if I understood everything.

I looked back at him and all I could muster for a response was, *"Dude …"*

Here we go again. Surgery. For a girl who had never had a broken bone or any surgery before (except the tonsillectomy I was awake for, the periodontal scrape, and the lumpectomy), I was racking up my score in a few short years with the hysterectomy, and now this.

The surgeon who gave me the news, Dr. W., would perform the surgery, but there was a different gynecological surgeon who would also be there, and I loved her!

She was young and bright and I trusted her. She was necessary because the chances were that this obstruction was caused by a return of the ovarian cancer. She spoke with me after the surgery and made me feel better about what had gone on. Dr. W. kept using the word "tumor" which somehow sounded more overwhelming to me. Dr. Axtell described it more as some cancer cells attaching to the intestines and constricting the flow. Either way, this meant cancer had come back and it also meant chemo. Really?

But this is why I loved Dr. Axtell so much. She said that my usual, local, oncologist would probably recommend the same chemo I had before because, in his mind, it worked. She said I should suggest a different chemo combo to him this time that had been shown to be as effective as the first one I had, but would have fewer side effects—including no hair loss!

She was right, my regular oncologist did suggest the same cocktail I had before and had not used the combo Dr. Axtell suggested. Then he made some additional treatment recommendations. I called Dr. Axtell who turned up her proverbial nose at those suggestions and urged me to be assertive. I was, and the doc went along with the suggestion, and so new chemo it would be.

But let's not jump too far ahead; I haven't mentioned anything about my hospital stay after the surgery. It was unbelievable.

Elena had called Scott and he came winging home as fast as he could from Denver, and was there when I was out of surgery and in a hospital room. Elena and Laurel were there, too. They took shifts with me. They were amazing and caring and so prepared with what to do, what to bring me, how to support Scott … life-savers!

I was in a bad way. I was out of it and in pain. I guess my gaunt, ashen visage gave Scott quite a scare.

There was only one thing that could make me feel a little better and that was a cold, wet rag on my forehead. Scott was re-soaking and re-wringing and replacing the cloth on my head constantly.

When Dr. W. came in to check on me and saw the cloth on my head, he said, "What's with the schmatta?" The word has stuck with us ever since. Isn't Yiddish the best? Schmatta is a rag or sometimes means clothing—popular in the garment district.

I was in the hospital for 11 days. My regular OB/GYN was there to check on me, too. He had said that the sooner I got out, the better, and he quoted the statistics about how the longer you stay in the hospital, the greater the risk of secondary infections and other demons. So, I tried! I wanted to get out as soon as possible. We were aiming for seven days.

Scott almost started a war with the doctors because he was so insistent that they all talk to each other, and he didn't feel they were. I asked him to cool it because I didn't want his anger to be taken out on me somehow. He was scared. I was too.

I was sick. I had never been so sick—even with the first surgery the four years before. I could not eat and I faced some of the things I'd dreaded most about being in a hospital. You guessed it, more nevers to confront. I'd seen those medical shows on TV! I knew what some of these things were, like the tube fed into the stomach through the nose. Never happen to me! You'd think I'd have learned that lesson by now, but I thought it and it manifested. Not once, but twice! Oh my God! That is an unpleasant sensation! And I won't even go into what was being pumped out of my stomach. Let's just say it rhymes with "vile" and … is … vile. When I was doing a bit better and they thought I'd gotten past the need for the tube, it was pulled out. Almost an equally unpleasant sensation.

Ah, but we weren't done. I started vomiting violently. Tube insertion take two. Oy! Give me my schmatta!

No permission to be released would be granted until I could eat solid food. I could order a choice off the hospital menu. Well, some of the meals sounded good, but when they were placed before me I could barely muster a bite. Ick! Much better in concept than reality. Even oatmeal. It's amazing the ways a perfectly good vegetable or grain or protein can be ruined.

Then came the day. I looked at Scott and said that I wanted a vanilla milkshake from the Stand, a nearby burger restaurant we liked. I had an appetite. I wanted something. It was a good sign. I could even watch out my window to see our car pull out of the parking lot below, and I counted the minutes, all the time watching out the window for the heralded return of Scott and the booty! Sure enough! I saw the car pull into the lot and Scott got out with a tall cup in his hand. There he came, there it was, and it was delicious! That's all it took—the magic potion. I was starting to feel good and starting to feel happy for the first time since before I first stepped into the ER.

I was released after some lovely training sessions with the ostomy nurse. Now *there's* a job! I had never heard of an ostomy or a stoma or an ostomy bag before, but this woman made her living in that field. Questions surrounding an ostomy, what it is and how you care for it, are even stranger than questions about sex or quantum physics. Actually, they're also kinda similar!

Luckily, Elena had helped a family member with the contraption before, so she was a big help with sizing and cutting the barrier and fastening on the bag. Wow, it's just like Tupperware. And the snapping-on sound is just as satisfying as when you're putting away your leftovers.

CHAPTER 24
LIFE HAPPENS

Scott had to get back to work. It had been so good to have him home to help me through my ordeal. The day after I left the hospital, he was on a plane again and would be gone from the end of August through the end of November. I knew I would miss him, and I completely lost track of which country he was in at any given time, and which "dude" was getting kidnapped and dropped somewhere so he could find his way out.

I was to go back to my life—home alone (except for my new friend, the ostomy bag), with the doggies and starting a whole new round of chemo.

I keep thinking about the saying, "life goes on." That just doesn't cover it for me. I saw how caught up I was in this whole storyline around Scott and our relationship. Then, despite how much bandwidth that whole script occupied, we were still presented with these other major events. What was the center ring? And what was going on in the other rings? And, in this three-ring circus, what was the main event? The ringmaster refused to answer my questions. So, along with life, the show must go on.

Enter the angels again—dear friends who would visit

me while I had chemo every month and would stay with me and bring me food and keep me company. The most powerful force in the universe: love, and it was all around me.

I was so thankful that I could still work. This was also good for my heart. I worked with wonderful people on projects that were fulfilling and rewarding—another source of love.

The chemo was going OK. Again, it was a new cocktail and the side effects were milder. I kept my hair; that was a plus. I still had the tough third day after treatment, but I got through it. Nausea, Elena's chicken soup, rest. It worked out. I also continued to exercise every day, and I focused on drinking more water.

I was now very happy with the naturopath I'd found and the supplements she had me taking. She knows her stuff and has always had a very positive attitude with me to this very day. I appreciate that! As before, I focused on keeping a positive attitude. Some doctors can keep their corner on the market of the glass half empty perspective.

Summer crept by this way. By October, I had a new distraction—drop foot. I noticed that, when I would go for a walk, my left foot would scuff along. I was shuffling with one foot, if that's possible. One day when I was barefoot, I made a point of trying to curl up my toes. Right foot was fine. Left foot ... hello? Is this thing on? My toes were not responding to the request. It is such a strange sensation to know you want your body to do something and not be able to do it!

My oncologist did not know what was causing this. He didn't think it was the chemo, though chemo is known for causing neuropathy. He approved me for Physical Therapy.

I showed up at the PT appointment to get a handle on what was going on so we'd know what to do about it. In the meantime, I had kept up my exercise, worked on toe curls and upped the L-Glutamine dose I'd been taking to prevent neuropathy. By the time I got to PT, things were already better and, after running me through a battery of walking and toe-pointing and other dance moves, the therapist released me and just encouraged me to keep up what I was doing. Eventually, no more drop foot. What was *that* about?!

As these sub-plots were playing out, I never stopped thinking about Scott, us, me and what was happening.

He wasn't home until late November when he only had a few weeks before he had to leave for another project at the end of December. When he was home, we'd dance around heavy topics at first because it just felt good to be together. But in time, the conversations would inevitably come around to "it," that subject that was always *always* lurking. I'd ask how he was doing and he would confess that the hijackings were still occurring. And I reverted to sometimes screaming my fears at the top of my lungs, my face coated with burning tears. I worried what the neighbors would think. How could they help but hear us?

For the most part, Scott was patient and tried to answer my questions and calm my fits. But he didn't always manage to stay calm and rational, either, and we'd both get caught in the blender. I wondered if there was a way to step over the chasm between us. Was there a compromise we could come to?

I was not interested in having Scott continue to lie to me or veil his answers so they would be more palatable to me. If we were partners in all this, then he should not have to look outside to find answers and acceptance.

We'd already done the long hair and earrings route. So, when he announced he wanted to shop for a purse, I offered to go with him to pick one out. We went to a couple of department stores and looked around. As with earring shopping, I felt that having some sense of control over things like this, I'd be able to maintain control over my life. I would suggest purses that I found on the racks that looked the least like a woman's purse as possible.

I found one that Scott also seemed to like. He'd offered up another choice, but it was big. A real commitment to a "purse!" We settled on the one I suggested and left the store. Baby steps.

CHAPTER 25
ALL I WANT FOR CHRISTMAS

2013 came to an end with little fanfare. My second cycle of chemo was done. I was doing pretty well and continued to work on regaining full health. More supplements from my naturopath, and I continued with the cannabis oil. But I still didn't like Cheech and Chong!

Christmas was around the corner. Scott was still away and going away on another project the day after Christmas.

This year, I was ready for Christmas. I spent the good part of the year knitting a sweater for Scott. I used to knit in the dark ages. My mother taught me when I was a teenager, and I did a couple things then, but nothing complicated. Now I was pulled to pick it up again. There is a great yarn shop near us where they sold anything you would ever need for knitting and crocheting. They have a huge banquet table at one end of the store where people can sit and knit and talk and get help. Some of the folks were regulars, and we got to know each other a bit. I say "folks" because, though it was mostly women, we had a wonderful 17-year-old boy who came and put many of us to shame with his knitting. It was a real old-fashioned knitting circle! This became a great hang-out for me. And I could feel productive about something in my life other than my work.

The sweater was complicated and beautiful. I had gone to the shop the year before because I wanted to make Scott a cable-knit Christmas stocking. When the shop's owner learned I hadn't knit in over 25 years, she suggested I start on a scarf. So I did. And it was good. I did more and more complicated scarves to get comfortable with the different stitches. They turned out great, which was fortunate because now I had hand-made Christmas presents to give! When I graduated to the stocking, I was ready. Well, with the help of the round-table! After that success, I knew I wanted to try a sweater.

I think I was just about as blown away as Scott at how well it came out. But best of all, it felt good to be doing something creative with my hands. Even if I was watching TV at night, I was also doing something constructive. And there's something so meditative about repetitive motion and the rhythm of the needles and the wrapping of the yarn. It's calming, primal even.

Because Scott would have so little time at home, I went to get our Christmas tree so it would be up when he arrived. My brother, Macky, and I found a beautiful tree! So tall and majestic! Our ornaments looked magnificent adorning it. And it was fun doing all that with my brother. Brought back old childhood memories.

Then came the annual Christmas Eve dinner with our dearest friends and family. Scott went wild, as usual! Timpano, and a feast for royalty.

Christmas day was perfect, and I was so happy to have a present for Scott that was such a surprise to him and something I had made myself. He had been the king of getting me the perfect gift for any occasion. I always felt behind on that score. So, this was a definite win! He loved the sweater. And it looked so good on him—a perfect fit and just the right splashes of blues and greens to electrify his hazel-blue eyes.

Little did I know, that was the last male gift I would give him.

Then, as quickly as he had come, he was gone again.

Our feast with friends came and went (even the leftover Timpano, eventually). Of course, the tree would have to come down, but I put it off as long as possible— not only because it was such a beautiful tree, but because I wanted the Christmas glow to go on and on. I was happy to have 2013 behind me—fears and loneliness and hospitals and questions. Should I say it? Yes, "Oh my!"

All I wanted for Christmas? My life ... back(?) Scott ... back(?). Certainly, my life had changed—from the inside— out and my marriage was definitely changing. Scott was changing, let's be real! How much more change would there be? That, I did not yet know. His hair an earrings were familiar now. I could barely call up what he looked like before. Sometimes I'd see pictures and would be shocked at the difference.

CHAPTER 26
WE CAN LAST FOREVER

2014, and Scott had been away on work for the greater part of three years by now. He was in Hawaii on a shoot from January to March and then back to Denver for another season of "Dude," from March to the end of April.

All this time away was starting to take its toll—at least on me.

When I was a little girl, my mother gave me a birthday card that I have not forgotten to this day. On the cover was a drawing of a cute little girl with a halo over her head, and the caption read, "You're an angel of a daughter who gets sweeter every year. And your halo never slips a bit!" And inside the halo was askew now, and it said, "Well, almost never, dear." I was getting to the "almost" stage. My halo was slipping. I was over being brave and up and so good through the surgeries and the cancer and the ostomy and the drop foot and my husband being away all the time, not to mention declaring he was a woman. Who thinks up this stuff? What had I done? How did this happen? I would squeeze my dogs tight at night and drench my pillow in my wailings and tears. I could feel my mind again want to take me to "why me?" If I had an answer, what would I do with it? How would it help me; how would it change anything?

Also, it was tough to wallow for long, because I do believe in the laws of karma, often defined as "what goes around comes around," or "As ye sow, so shall ye reap." I reminded myself how important it is to be aware of where I put my attention, so I surveyed my life and had to admit that I was the most loved wife on the planet. Whatever else was going on with Scott, he was the most loving husband ever.

I had friends who were the definition of the word, "friendship," a job I loved with people I loved, I had our treehouse and two perfect dogs. I had a body that, despite all it was being subjected to, was holding up amazingly well—taking the blows and bouncing back. Focusing on the positive made me feel better, much better than focusing on loss.

Scott and I were coming up on our 25th Anniversary on April 29, 2014.

For 25 years (actually 27, counting the two years we lived together) my life was entwined in his. I could not imagine life without him. And what if all this did lead to those scenes that had scared me so much before from "Normal" or "Orange is the New Black?" Well, what if that was where things were going?

Over this whole span of time since Scott first told me about being a woman, the process felt like peeling an onion. One belief after another, one concept after another had to be held up to the light and examined. But if it sounds as though I was taking two steps forward and one step back, I was. I kept cycling through the stages of "I can't take this" and "maybe we can make it work." But more than a cycle, I'd call it a spiral, because I felt like I was gradually moving more and more into the acceptance stage, despite my fear and denial stages.

Now I was starting to think more about the other side of the coin—Scott's side. Could I be facing a fate even worse than all that I had been conjuring up before this point? Scott was gone so much, I sensed a distance. He had made a parallel life for himself with a whole new community of friends and co-workers. New experiences. New activities. New ...?

New feelings? About me. About us.

Sometimes our good-night phone calls would be strained. He'd be out with the crew and couldn't talk long because he had stepped outside the restaurant to talk to me and had to get back. But he sounded distracted. More and more, I'd call him at night and the calls would go to voicemail. I'd call again and again. I'd text. No answer. And, when he would never have been concerned in the past about calling me too late, I now was not getting that good night kiss call at all. I'd find myself, phone next to my bed, checking it constantly. Was it working? Was the ringer off? If I fell asleep, I'd wake up continually during the night—every hour on the hour. And I'd keep calling, even in those wee hours, knowing it was even later for Scott in Colorado.

Had my resistance to completely understanding what he was going through created a rift? Was there someone else there in Denver who did understand him better, who could relate to him in ways I hadn't? Could I could lose him? He had always been rock solid about us, about our staying together. He was firm and resolved and steadfast and always said "forever." But his life was transforming from the inside out. He had told me that some things would never happen, and they did. So if never could change, maybe forever could.

That word is in so many songs, right? Songs can worm their way into our mind and heart and leave an imprint there that can last for years. I bet you can recall songs that correspond to a specific time in your life right now. Peter Gabriel's "In Your Eyes" was *our* song. I walked down the aisle to it. Whenever it would come on my playlist, I'd tear up.

I didn't listen to music a whole lot, usually only when I was doing our bookkeeping and had to have something fun happening while I was in my desk chair doing stuff that was anything but fun. The first time "We Can Last Forever" by Chicago came on, it stopped my heart. The more I listened to the lyrics, the more I connected to the song. The melody is haunting and uplifting all at once. I listened over and over, and I kept having the thought that this is how I felt—it was certainly how I wanted to feel. When I thought that what we were going through could possibly really split us up—that I could lose the love of my life—I felt a hollowness inside, deeper than I had ever known.

I needed to take a long, hard look at what was really important to me. When I caught myself wondering if I could lose Scott to someone else, I felt frightened and my blood ran cold. Having that carpet pulled out from under me was even worse to imagine than what I'd been trying to deal with over the previous few years.

I emailed an MP3 of the song to Scott. I wanted him to hear it, to drink it in, to feel as connected through it as I did, and as we both did when we heard "In Your Eyes."

Here are the lyrics:

Don't turn away 'cause there is something I just wanna say
I need you to stay, don't ask me why 'cause I don't even
know how I gave you my heart, I gave it all to you
Now there's no way that I can lose

Every little look inside your eyes
Is all it takes to make me realize, we can last forever

With every little moment we can share
Gonna let you know how much I care, I'll always be there

Don't walk away 'cause there is something I just gotta say
I love you today, just ask me why, you're all I'll ever need
Now that you're in my life, I really think you should know
That I never wanna let you go

Every little look inside your eyes
Is all it takes to make me realize, we can last forever
Every little moment we can share
Gonna let you know how much I care, love lift us away

We can last forever

Every little look inside your eyes
Is all it takes to make me realize, we can last forever
Every little moment we can share
Gonna let you know how much I care.

I thought this would touch Scott; reach him. He was so into music. His whole life had its own soundtrack. And best of all, he was a Chicago fan. But, though Scott liked the song, I don't think it struck him the way I was hoping it would: that it would bring us back into the rarified air that had been ours alone—our life, our love, our music.

Was I reaching out to him too late? Was Scott drifting away? Finding other friends or ... I mean, after all, I hadn't been very understanding. Or open. Or accepting. Or even affectionate.

My thoughts were constant and relentless. This ache in my heart that I could somehow lose Scott was making me wrack my brain for answers. What were the most important aspects of our relationship, our marriage? Had I really been willing to give it all up on a technicality? OK, I just had to toss that in there. A little gallows humor?

I clung to the things that made me feel safe. I focused on trust. Though I was questioning Scott, I reminded myself of his declarations of love, his guarantee that we would always be together. I had no facts to confirm he was drifting away, just my own imaginings trapped in the vacuum of my own mind. I had to allow that I could be wrong. I wanted to be wrong!

CHAPTER 27
A SILVER YEAR

Scott and I had very little time to be together or to talk at all. He was out of the country until a couple days before our Silver Anniversary on April 29th. I think he was in Finland. Or was it Romania?

And I had the challenge of what to get the man in silver? I started my search weeks before. I wanted something he would love and preferably have with him all the time—something he could wear? I kept picturing an I.D. bracelet. Oh brother! I went from jewelry store to kiosk, but the choices were, well, not choices. I checked the internet. I wasn't sure what I wanted, but I knew what I didn't want, and that was all the ones I was looking at.

I spent hours in a nearby mall one day and visited every store that carried jewelry, including the department stores. Ugh! Nothing! I was about to give up when I wandered into David Yurman, a very classy shop with his original designs displayed in beautiful glass cases with LED lights that made every ring and necklace and bracelet shimmer like royal treasure. The service was impeccable. A lovely young woman named Sarah helped me, and we talked about what I was looking for. They didn't have I.D.

Bracelets on display, but, when I asked, she said they did have a couple in the back. She brought out for me to look at. Yes! I found a beautiful one! It was very original looking. I loved the tight weave in the silver chain, and the area for engraving was classy and a bit rounded looking. The chain was strong, but didn't scream masculine. I loved it. Woohoo! Now, what to have the engraving say?

I struggled with this one. I still didn't know where we were headed, or how far Scott would end up going with a transition, but I just didn't have the heart to reinforce him as Scott. Even having his initials seemed a bit cold. I was at a loss. I wanted it to mean something special to him; to us. But what?

Though I didn't know what our destination was, I knew there was one common denominator: our love. I had loved this person for over 25 years, and he had taught me so much about love. He was at my side through discovering ovarian cancer and all that ensued. And he also had trusted my instincts and the way I wanted to deal with the disease. No pressure, just support and love; just massaging my bald head and aching legs. Cooking for me ... everything. I was grateful for what we had, for all our experiences, for our affection and intimacy, for supporting the work I wanted to do ... there was so much to be grateful for. And there was the golden strand of love that intersected it all.

I was shifting a bit more. I wasn't sure how far I could go, how much I could accept, but my focus was more on our untaintable love.

And then I got it!

Since our early days together, when one of us would say, "I love you," the other would answer, "And I, thee!" As shorthand in texts or emails, we would sign, 314 (representing the number of letters in those three words).

That was ours; that was us. So, there was my answer. Not his name, not any name, but an affirmation of our love. Twenty-five years married? That deserved honoring and celebrating no matter what was to come.

Once I sent that information by email to Sarah, she sent me engraving samples. They seemed a bit blocky. I asked if they had one that was more scripty-looking. She said no, but that she would talk to the engraver. They came up with a perfect solution. There was a way to use an italics version of the font I liked, and he was fine with doing that for the bracelet.

This was a fairly expensive piece of jewelry, but I was enjoying my un-skin-flinty self coming out. As with the custom-knit Christmas stocking and sweater I'd made for Scott, I was enjoying the process of coming up with great, original gifts that required planning and meaning.

Scott worked it out to come home for a couple of days so we could celebrate our anniversary. Then he would be off to Africa!

Because our anniversary would be the day before he had to leave, we agreed to go to a restaurant we liked the night before to celebrate. And that is where we exchanged gifts.

I opened mine first. Two gifts. One was a beautiful silver bracelet—a very original weave of wide silver strands. Almost like an I.D. bracelet without the I.D. piece. And also a necklace—a combination of different silver strands and chains with a round pendant hanging from them. It had layered shapes representing a silver moon with a brass sun on top of that. Very unique and beautiful. Naturally, I was quite blown away by the synchronicity of the bracelet! Yikes! These were old pieces that Scott had been given by a good friend he had come to know who lived in the country outside of Denver with her husband and various animals, including deer who visited regularly. He was visiting them and told them our silver anniversary was coming up and he still hadn't found anything he wanted to give me. Alicia didn't waste a moment and went to her jewelry case to pull out items for Scott to look at and choose from. When he admired both pieces, she promptly handed them both to him; no questions asked. A beautiful and generous gift.

So, there we were in the restaurant. After receiving— and instantly putting on—my gifts, I handed Scott my gift to him. It was gift-wrapped in a beautiful box with a velour bag inside holding its precious contents. Scott was taken aback by the bracelet, and it fit so perfectly—looked beautiful on his wrist. And we laughed about our almost matching bracelets! We agreed to never take them off. He was touched by the *314,* especially when I explained how I'd made the decision to have that engraved on the bracelet instead of initials or names, and that I had picked the bracelet because it was not one of those clunky I.D. bracelets that were obviously made for a man.

We both could see that I was at least recognizing where Scott was at and not wanting to shackle him to an identity that ... might not fit anymore.

The next night was April 29, the actual anniversary date. I'd suggested that we just stay home and be together, since we'd gone out to dinner the night before. That seemed fine until early evening when Scott said he just couldn't take it and had to do something celebratory, still. He said he'd figure something out and was going to surprise me with the restaurant choice. I was just to put on something "somewhat dressy" and be ready to leave at a certain time.

Once we were in the car, we took off heading west and I started my guessing game to see if I could figure out which restaurant we were heading to. We took some crazy turns and rerouting. I eventually knew he wasn't lost, as first proclaimed, but was maybe trying to confuse me. We headed back east toward Ventura Boulevard, and ended up parking near our favorite Indian restaurant. That was fine with me, though I'd expected he would have tried for something new and different.

When we walked in the door, I received a huge shock!

As my eyes adjusted to the light, I saw some familiar faces—people seated at tables right inside the door. Great friends from San Diego! What?! My mouth hung open in dazed amazement as one face after the other came into focus—dear, dear friends … face after face … people from far and wide, including my brother and his daughter whom Scott had flown in from San Francisco! There were about forty people in all! No, none of this could be real, yet here they all were—to celebrate our 25th! Generous, wonderful friends, some we'd known for decades, some for 10 years or less. But all there because Scott had called and arranged everything long distance, well ahead of time! He pulled this all together from his office in Denver as well as by sat phone on location in Romania.

He'd arranged with the restaurant to provide a delicious Indian buffet, and there were flat bowls on all the tables with gardenias floating in them (our anniversary tradition. Scott always got me a gardenia blossom on each anniversary for every year we'd been married. That became an amazing feat from Poland one year). And the cake, ah the cake! Our wedding cake came in three tiers: carrot cake, dark chocolate, and lemon cake with mango filling. Scott had gotten our favorite bakery to make three cakes to replicate what we'd had on our wedding day.

OK, now, do I need to go on about how romantic and thoughtful and special this husband was?

What a fun and memorable night! It was full of love

and laughter, sweet reunions and magical connections of our dear expanded family who were now enjoying getting acquainted with each other. Everyone catching up, chiming in, swapping Scott and Marcy stories and our shared histories. My Matron of Honor, Debra, was there, and a couple of Scott's Best Men. Remember, he did not want one Best Man and then groomsmen. All nine were Best Men!

It was definitely over too soon! The one consolation was that three of our San Diego friends had decided to stay that night in a hotel, and we got together for breakfast the next morning.

Without a doubt, we have *the* most loving, caring, generous, thoughtful, loyal friends in the whole world! I hope they all know that this journey of mine (ours) would not have been possible without their support and wisdom.

CHAPTER 28
GOOD NEWS/BAD NEWS

After our magical anniversary, I felt a slight breath of fresh air.

Scott went off the next day to Africa which was only the beginning of his traveling to other far reaches of the planet. He would be gone through the early part of July, through my birthday on the 5th.

We had talked about having Scott come home for my birthday, but I said that was just too much—too short, too expensive ... don't bother. So, he told me he'd been invited to a 4th of July party and it would be so deep in the Colorado mountains, he might not have cell reception. We wished each other a happy 4th, happy birthdays (his is on the 9th) and said, "ciao."

As soon as we hung up, I was sad. Though we had had such a glorious anniversary celebration, I was still uneasy. We had not had the time to talk; really talk.

I wanted to get to the bottom of this and what it was going to mean to our world specifically.

In some ways, because I was seeing more and more coverage of the subject of transgender in news and in several TV shows and movies, I was at least seeing this was not *the* most strange and foreign thing in the world. It was more prevalent than I had thought, and this was something that was helped by Scott being away. I could watch shows, read up, learn more and become a bit more accepting of the transgender world without worrying about him discovering me while I was doing my homework.

And I missed him. Especially over the holiday of July 4th, 5th and 9th which had always been a celebration week for us.

July 4th arrived. I had no plans. How pathetic. About mid-day, the doorbell rang. I went to the door and saw a large box in the carport that had a note on it that said, "Woodland Hills Florist." Wow! He must have sent me a tree! I bet it was a lemon tree, because we'd talked about getting one. There was a ribbon around the box with a big bow in the front, and the note also said to open it immediately. The end of the ribbon had a "start here" note on it. So, I did. I pulled on the ribbon which had me walk around the box until it revealed a cut out door at the front that opened when I tugged a little harder. There, inside the box ... No! Yes! No! It's wishful thinking! It was Scott, smiling back at me! I hugged him and then hit him and hugged him again saying, "I'm so powerful!"

Our friends, Elena and Laurel, came out from their respective hiding places nearby, laughing and giggling with glee—very willing accomplices in this mad plan to get Scott home for my birthday. They got me but good! I hear stories like this, but I didn't think it would happen to me. Though, Lord knows, I was kinda wishing for it. Wow! The perfect birthday present. And Scott would be home for a week.

And then, another present followed. It turned out to be not the best gift.

I went to the hospital on July 10th so the surgeons could "take down" my ostomy. Really? "Take down?"

What a strange term. I could see "reverse" or some such description, but … take down?

I had been through the necessary tests ahead of time. The doctors wanted a scan of the area to see if the take down looked feasible. Ah, back to drinking the contrast fluid and lying on a cold table for the x-ray. They said they didn't have to put the wand in the ostomy this time, which did happen on my last photo shoot; they'd just go in the back door with fluid which I was to try to hold in as long as possible (almost impossible). Unpleasant, but they finally said they got what they needed and I could get dressed.

I was half dressed in the bathroom and they knocked and asked me to come back. The radiologist needed a better film. There was a dark area he was hoping to get a better look at. OK, back on the table; now I'm shivering and cold. Everything is soaking wet. So, another x-ray, another "thank-you-you-can-get-dressed," and another knock on the bathroom door after I had my clothes on. The tech apologized profusely, as did the radiologist, but they just needed to try again. And this time, they would also have to go in through the ostomy. Oh joy! I'll spare you the details. You're welcome!

OK, that was the last re-take, thank goodness, because it was just too much to lie on that table, shivering even harder than before and having the cold, sticky contrast fluid they were pumping into me flow out all over me and onto the table where I was lying. I just don't know how people take even more pain and unpleasantness in the course of getting medical care. Finally, I could go home and come back on the 10th for the surgery.

Dear Dr. W. was there again (schmatta doctor) and my favorite gynecology oncology surgeon, Dr. Axtell, since the original condition stemmed from the ovarian cancer).

Same surgery prep routine. I had a different

anesthesiologist from my previous surgeries, and she explained everything very clearly. She told me I'd probably remember everything up to entering the operating room. I told her that the time before, I conked out a few seconds after being wheeled out of pre-op. She said that wasn't really true, because I would have had to help the medical team move me from the gurney to the operating table. So, I was awake, it's just that propofol is designed to block the memory, not "knock you out." Really! Wow! This time, I tried to stay awake and aware longer, just to see if I could remember more this time. I did ... I could see the lights overhead as they wheeled me on my bumpy ride to the OR, just like in the movies, and could hear the double swinging doors as we passed over the bumpy threshold. After that? Nada!

As I was coming to in recovery, I saw Scott and Dr. Axtell who said they couldn't take down the ostomy because there were some cancerous nodules in my abdomen, and they just didn't want to do anything while that was still there. They only did a laparoscopy to get those results, so my recovery would not be as long and tedious as it might have been. Dr. Axtell recommended another round of chemo once I recovered from the surgery. My other oncologist later told me there was no way of knowing whether those cells were new or just left over after my previous treatment. I felt hopeful with that prospect.

Disappointing news from the surgery, nevertheless. I was looking forward to not having Junior (my name for the ostomy contraption) hanging off my abdomen anymore, but there we were! It may have been right then that I was starting to resign myself to not ever(?) doing a take-down surgery. Dr. Axtell had said that, even if I were clear of cancer, if it were to come back and affect my intestines that way again, I might have to have another colostomy. Uh, no thank you! As things go, this was not the most awful thing in the world. And there are some advantages. You figure them out! It is amusing when I do occasionally pass gas, because people hear the familiar sound, but are dumbfounded by the direction it seems to come from. It's the little things that keep me smiling, ya know?

And this was just early July? It feels like these past couple of years had been jam-packed with tests and lessons and trials. The winds of change keep wafting through our lives with new challenges and questions. My question in response again is, "Really?!"

Four days after my non-surgery surgery, my oldest brother, Macky, went into the hospital for a triple bypass. See what I mean? And of course, the hospital was in Orange County, over an hour from home. Those were fun visits. LA traffic is a big factor when trying to drive anywhere. And, if you don't time it just right around commute times, lunchtime, "Friday night light," airport traffic and accidents, the time on the freeway can grow exponentially!

Luckily, he recovered very well and we were all relieved—especially him! It was serendipity that he found out about his heart the way he did. He went in for a physical and the doctor he saw told him that he should not go home, but that she was admitting him to the hospital that day and he would be scheduled for surgery. We shudder when we think of what might have happened if that physical hadn't happened when it did.

Macky's recovery was on track, so it was my turn again, and I started chemo on August 13th. We were doing carbo/doxil again, since it had worked before and had fewer negative side-effects than the carbo/taxol. I sure liked keeping my hair. It was finally getting long again, which I prefer. Me in short hair? Please!

Yup! Just over half-way through the year and 2014 was already a doozy!

CHAPTER 29
PROVIDENCE, IN MORE WAYS THAN ONE

Anticipation was building for a trip in September. After reconnecting with three of my best friends from elementary school several years before, the four of us agreed to get together for a long weekend every two years. Two of us lived on the West Coast—LA and Carmel—and the other two lived on the East Coast—Providence and Charlottesville. This is the year when we were coming full circle to Providence where it all began those eight years before when we made the pledge to keep meeting. All of us were married, and spouses were always included. It was a treat to see how our husbands were also now forming their own friendships separate from just being there to get a kick out of the four of us women and our high-pitched laughter and stories of the old days and our school escapades. We were also making headway on catching up to present day, sharing what our lives were like since the end of the 9th grade when we went our separate ways to boarding school. We continued to catch up on the stories of what life was *really* like for us back then in the age of not so innocent—alcoholic parents, abusive parents, family crises and secrets all swept under Persian rugs. We knew some of these things about each other's lives, and we were surprised to hear some other things. Shocked even! How did we not see what our friend was going through?! What might we have done to help, if we'd only known? Revealing, touching, frightening, in some cases. And so, these long weekends were filled with laughter and tears and memories and shocks and wonderful outings and local tours.

The Providence weekend dates were set well in advance—September 25th-28th. I had arranged with Christie that Scott and I would stay a couple more days and leave on the 30th. I'm so glad I did!

So amazing as always! Fantastic food every day, including whole lobster, and cucumber and butter sandwiches and a gorgeous day touring around Block Island culminating in the most decadent ice cream shoppe. I was back east; there was only one ice cream flavor for me in that case—black raspberry. There is just nothing like it. Sorry. And I'm not much of a fruit ice cream or sorbet girl. But black raspberry is the tongue-tingling exception. I was a happy camper! But I'm getting ahead of myself here.

Scott had been on a shoot in Alaska for the weeks since I got out of the hospital. He flew home the night of the 24th and we got on a plane to Boston's Logan airport the next day.

I was wondering how "the girls" were going to respond to Scott's long hair and earrings. When we first arrived in Providence and he wanted to change clothes, I saw that his toe nails were painted. Even he was wondering how that would be received. I was taken aback; this was news to me, but no one said anything.

I ached to be able to talk to my friends, anyone, about what was going on with us. I was embarrassed. Now there were reasons for me to feel separate or isolated from my old friends. My "normal," wonderful husband was looking very different. I just wasn't sure how this would fly. We girls were all originally New Englanders—known for the tendency to be more conservative in mores and styles. Would they chalk it up to Scott being "Hollywood?" Maybe. But I was uncomfortable with my own discomfort. I didn't like feeling that I might be left out somehow myself, that we might be talked about. And that old companion, resentment, came to visit again. Why did Scott have to do this? Why did he, and therefore, I, have to go down this road?

Agreed, I was more accepting of his changes. I had worked on preparing myself for what seemed to be the inevitable. But one of the problems was that the bar of the inevitable kept getting moved. Scott's female expression was sneaking out more and more as time went on.

And that's the strange thing about a bar moving when you don't expect it to, or when someone tells you they're done and then they're not. You don't now know where it all will end. You thought this was the finish line. OK, great! Then, the finish line gets pushed out further ... and then again ... and again ...

Scott was away so much of this year and the couple years before. Through all the clawing and scratching at the idea of Scott being transgender, through all my fears and anger and hurt, I was also well aware that I missed him. Though I wondered if I could stay through this whole possible trans-form-ation, I was leaning more toward the idea of staying than going. I had visualized what my life would be like without My Love, and it was not a pretty picture.

But here, with my old, dear friends, deep-seated feelings were coming up—the schoolgirl clique fears that I was not fitting in, that my friends wouldn't understand, that I'd be at worst, alone, at best, different. Ah, those preteen years of best friends on the ins and outs. Being back with those friends, with that familiar dynamic—It didn't seem to matter how many decades had passed—I felt like that young girl again, not sure of my future, of what I wanted, of where I wanted to go to school, of who I wanted to be. I used to envy people who seemed sure of who they were and what they wanted, who seemed to breeze through life with confidence and knowing. I had achieved a lot in my life up until now. I had answers to a lot of my biggest questions. I had a spiritual perspective that gave me solace and a trusted compass. But there were times that wasn't enough in this new phase of my life. And I was right back in the 8th grade, learning.

It appeared my fears on this trip were unfounded. Everyone was clicking along quite nicely, and there was a wonderful air of lightness and fun that wove through our time together. Sunday came too fast, and the other two couples said their "goodbyes" and headed off to their next destinations.

As we closed the front door, it was now just Scott and me, Christie and Jeff. Christie turned to Scott and said, "So what is this, Scott? Are you getting in touch with your feminine side?" Ah, that's my dear, perspicacious, soon-to-retire therapist friend.

Scott sighed and said that this was a bigger discussion, could we go sit and talk. So, we got a beverage and sat at the dining room table. And Scott proceeded to explain that he was a woman. It came out about that instantly and matter-of-factly. There it was! It was said. It was out. He, I mean she, was out! Just like that. No turning back, no fudging that this was a Hollywood look, no feminine side or anima/animus explanations or deflections. A woman. Plain and simple. Well, not at all plain and not *at all* simple! But out, nonetheless.

Something happened inside me in that moment. Having this out in the open for the first time, at least for me, I felt a touch of relief. At least it wasn't a secret anymore. There was a glimmer of a promise that I was no longer alone. I wasn't boxed in by my own silence, and maybe there were friends that I could turn to in this after all ... people I could talk to, confide my feelings to, be supported and counseled by. At this point, I preferred the idea of talking with friends more than counselors. That hadn't worked so well for me, if you remember. With Christie, there was the bonus of her being a best friend *and* a counselor! How fortunate was I?

And so, Christie and Jeff listened. They were surprised, but they were also compassionate. Christie and I went to the kitchen to refill our glasses and she asked how I was doing. I truly don't remember what I said. It was just such a great feeling to be able to talk to someone, talk to my best friend from years ago. One thing that stood out to me that day, and I have held onto it since, is that Christie said, "Well, I don't think this means you have to split up, do you?"

I had been stumbling and tiptoeing and bush-whacking my way through this jumble of feelings and fears and questions for about five years at this point. Huh! Well, I hadn't left yet, and my heart had belonged to Scott for 27 years. I got reassurance from what Christie said. It calmed me and helped me to feel less alone. The word for what I got is ... permission. That may sound strange. But I think much of the undercurrent of my fears had been related to fearing people would judge me, judge us. Having Christie so warmly and matter-of-factly say what she did about our not having to split made me feel I had an ally, someone who didn't feel that this was such a huge issue that a couple should break up over it. I guess it seemed suddenly doable.

It was the ease that came out in her words and tone. It was a question, but felt like a rhetorical one. I used the word, "permission," and it did strike me that way—that I had Christie's permission, or maybe "blessing" is a better word, to stay in this all the way. OK, right! We didn't have to split. That meant we had other options open to us.

Christie and Jeff were so great. I think, when we finally asked Jeff what he was thinking, because he had been rather quiet, he said something to the effect of, "I don't care," meaning, it didn't matter to him if Scott was a man or woman. He cared about us, and it just wasn't that big a deal.

There was one more thing that Christie said that day that has stayed with us as a guiding light ever since. She said that, as long as we treated this with dignity, we would be Okay. Dignity. A powerful word that shined in our lives going forward and ever since.

We did find out that there had been some discussion about Scott among the group over the weekend when we weren't around. They wondered what was going on with Scott and raised the question with each other. That tugged on my "hate to be on the outside" cord a bit, but I understood. Really, how could I be surprised?

And so, this epic reunion came to a close with a bonus sense of closure.

I felt bolstered. We had allies as a couple now, in this new way of being a couple.

A new start ... at least a new chapter.

And, though this ended our visit to Providence, Providence would play a big role in our lives down the road.

CHAPTER 30
IF YOU THINK I'M CONFUSED, YOU SHOULD SEE *ME*!

As soon as we got home from Providence, Scott was on a plane to Alaska. This show was going to take him to five different locations at the farthest reaches of the state, and he'd have to travel back and forth between them regularly. Planes and boats and helicopters and snowmobiles. He was disappointed that "Dude, You're Screwed" was not picked up for a third season, but it meant he was available to take this other job as showrunner.

Our time with Christie and Jeff had somehow softened and opened us more to each other. Scott was feeling a little bit safer and bolder about telling me about what had been going on for him. Much of it was over the phone since he was gone for a few months yet again, but I also think that the phone made it a bit easier. We had a shred of telephonic fabric to hide behind that protected us from looking into each other's eyes for the toughest questions and answers.

And so, Scott told me some more facts about his many months when he was in Denver over the two years leading up to this.

Much of it was hard for me to hear, but I just had to. I wanted to know everything! I needed to close that gap between being on the outside and the inside.

I gripped the handrails as the Denver stories kept coming. Scott had been seeking out LGBTQ groups there, making friends, going out with them …dressed in women's clothes and going to bars; going out on the town. Even getting flirted with by men. Oh, shoot me now! Really? What was I supposed to do with this information? "No," he insisted, of course nothing "happened." But now I had these images floating around in my head.

I literally could not fathom that my mate, my husband, my … everything … could manage to not only do this, but get away with it! Manage to keep all this a secret … manage to have such a distinct life separate from ours; separate from me. I'm sorry, but I thought it was a big deal for me to go out to the knitting shop and join the knitting circle of people there. I thought that was about as outside our life as I could stand to be without Scott. Ha! Right?

If I went out with friends, got together with friends, they were our friends—not people Scott had never met. I was predictable. There was nothing about me for him to worry about. I was safe. Ah, but he still didn't feel safe with me, safe enough to share his deepest feelings. Maybe my previous screaming and crying about his being trans made him feel that there was no place to go where he could fully trust me, share with me, include me.

Who were these new friends? Would I like them if I met them? Were they leading Scott down the proverbial primrose path? Would there be a point of no return, or was he already there?

Before, there were the times when I wondered whether I might leave, but now I wondered if Scott would leave. Maybe our marriage just wasn't right for him now, enough for him. Maybe I wasn't enough. He loved me, had always proclaimed his love for me, but he was also stepping inexorably into a new world, and the possibility was striking me that I might just not fit in that world, even if I wanted to.

I truly hadn't thought about sexuality and what these changes might mean to us. There's gender and there's sexuality, and they have nothing to do with each other. Many people are confused about that, and it often leads to a huge misunderstanding and even judgment of trans people because some think of it as a choice. It's not a choice, any more that one's sexual orientation is a choice.

If Scott is really a woman and loves me, he's (she's) a lesbian. If "she's" a lesbian, does that mean I'm a lesbian? Or could Scott be interested in men? I went down every dark alley in my mind, I can assure you. Did Scott want to do some experimentation to be sure?

Was that bar moving again? How far was it going this time?

Images haunted me. I imagined these nights out. I thought about all those nights when I would call and get voicemail and not even get a call back.

There I was at home. Alone. My own version of Madame Defarge ... knitting away at the shroud I was trying on for size. The shroud of my marriage?

But between thoughts, there was the rest of life. I was in my third round of chemo which finally ended on December 11th. The Oncologist suggested I could have one more treatment, but that it was up to me and I said, "No. I'm done."

From October 20th to November 2nd, between chemo treatments, I had the wonderful distraction of a production project out of town. I jumped in with both feet and all smiles. I was the director on a company's event being held for their staff. My production chops were dragged out of storage and I was back in it, just like riding a bike. My goal was for everyone involved—crew, talent, audience—to have fun! And we did. I received such heart-warming input from people that they loved working on the project with me, that it was fun, and that they learned a lot. I could not have wished for more. And to be there among friends, colleagues and familiar faces was an elixir for my soul.

Then ... November already?!! Thanksgiving! Yikes, I don't know what I did for Thanksgiving! I do know what Scott did—a cooking extravaganza with his crew in Alaska. This is all very detailed in Scott's book, right down to crab leg and blueberry turkey dressing. And I later heard "she" dressed as herself, too. And the crew was unfazed. Really? What was the world coming to?

One thing, I guess, it is coming to is "she" from "he."

I might as well make the pronoun switch at this juncture.

Am I now seeing this as inevitable? Elvis has left the building. The worm has turned. The train has left the station. The ship has pulled away from the dock. The die is cast. The jig is up. This is fun! Find some more with me! The tables have turned. The time has come. 'Tis the season. The horse has left the stable. The fat lady has sung. Don't dip your pen in the company ink. Oh, wait! Sorry, that one doesn't belong here, but it is business advice my dad gave me at an early age, and I've always liked it.

While we're sharing parental wisdom, the title for this chapter came from something my mother used to say, "If you think I'm confused, you should see me!" Seemed to fit where I was at. And boy, does that ever come into play with the pronoun game! A game that many people lose. Over and over and over....

CHAPTER 31
THE END OF A YEAR-A

Christmas, 2014 is around the corner. What a year!

I had started my Christmas shopping for ... Okay, her.

Scott will come home for a few days on December 10th from Alaska, then off to another shoot from December 14th through the 20 th. She'd be home for five days so we could have Christmas, would leave the day after Christmas and be gone into January.

There'd basically only be time for Scott to unpack, do laundry, make Christmas cookies and candies, and repack for a different climate, now in Canada.

When I was Christmas shopping, I ordered two beautiful mail-order tops from a catalogue company for Scott. Women's tops. Granted, they were nice tunics, but didn't scream woman. I was taking baby steps still, but I was taking steps nonetheless. I also made her a couple of pairs of earrings. This was different from the earring shopping we had done early on. These were from me to her. I picked out the design and the beads and charms and made two pair. This was my way of showing that I was turning the corner. This was a huge deal for me, and I knew it would be a big deal for her.

This was the second year in a row that I also got our Christmas tree, since Scott would only be home a few days. I wanted the tree up when she got home and for as long as possible, as we'd always done.

And this Christmas was going to be extra special! Two of my three brothers were going to be here with us, along with brother Doug's two daughters, Sophie and Rosie.

This would also be the beginning of several months when Macky would be coming to live with us once he was done with a stint in a half-way house. He had made some very poor choices in a white-collar crime sort of way, and had done his time, as the phrase goes. We wanted to help him get back on his feet—and preferably away from Marin County where it had all gone south for him. So, we offered him a room in our treehouse. His half-way house months were almost over, and he'd be moving in as of Christmas Day. Hey! It wasn't as if we had anything else do to!

Obviously, we needed to let him know what had been going on with us. So, we invited him over and sat him down to have "the talk." I wish you could meet him. First, let me say that all four of us McVickars, my brothers and I, have a lot in common: our childhood together packed with great memories, good parents, and a strong underpinning of humor all along the way. We were alike in many ways; and not in others.

I'm sure the news was a shock to Macky, though he took it very calmly. But transgender was not a topic that I think he knew much about at all. So there were (and sometimes still are) questions and even the inappropriate joke or two. And don't get me started on pronouns! He tries. He often succeeds, but.…

After all, when you've had a brother-in-law for over 25 years, to suddenly be told it's your sister-in-law is a complete shock to the system.

Now this telling people thing was a little more comfortable. We'd told Jeff and Christie and now Macky. No one's head spun around, no doors were slammed, so maybe this wasn't as bad as I'd feared. Maybe this wasn't so completely strange to everyone; maybe we weren't so different that we'd be ridiculed and deserted. The magic shawl of dignity was gently wrapped around our shoulders and life as we knew it was not ending.

Now, Laurel and Elena are friends whom I'd been wanting to talk to about this, practically from day one. They are a loving, dear, couple who had been our guardian angels through my illness as well as those great friends you just want to have dinner with and talk for hours. We love them with all our hearts and cannot get enough of them. I hadn't spoken to them about Scott however, because I felt this was something for us to do together. Now that Scott was home and we were starting to tell people, it was as good a time as any. So we had them over.

Scott was dressed in a more feminine way and had on some make-up. They noticed. I noticed, too—that she looked different, softer. The make-up played up more feminine features in her face. I had to admit she looked pretty. We told Laurel and Elena the news. We hugged and sat together for a long exchange of questions and answers and warm support.

We had to cover a lot of turf on the "what's next" side of the coin. Those questions are always in the forefront. Scott was about to return to Canada for the last part of the shoot she was directing. How would she dress now?

I just was not ready to see Scott "out in the world" (yes, a play on words). And in the work setting? I knew most of the people she was working with; that's where I was on my last project, and I didn't think I could handle the fall out. Laurel and Elena chuckled when Scott said she could fly under the radar and wouldn't be outed if she wore slacks and a jacket.

They were right. Let's just say the radar had a much wider range than we imagined. And Canada turned out to be a pivotal time in Scott's coming out.

That time gave her great strength and a new footing.

But let's not fly past Christmas so fast!

CHAPTER 32
WITH ALL THE TRIMMINGS

Though we only had a few days where we were together at Christmas, it was a magical time.

Our tree was more beautiful than ever, though we do say that every year.

Having two of my three brothers here, as well as two of my three nieces, was so great—a huge slumber party! Bodies everywhere, and I loved it!

Christmas was a big deal when we were growing up. My mother decorated like crazy; my grandmother and I baked pies and cookies; the family was together, including my brothers who were home from boarding school. I joined that club at fifteen.

We had wonderful traditions, and it was always such a rite of passage when we were old enough to stay up and help wrap presents. When it was my turn to join the secret wrappers, we only had my younger brother, Doug, to hide presents from. The game got quite tricky when it turned out that some of us were also wrapping presents for others in the room, right under their noses!

It seemed that every year included at least one gift that required assembly. My dad and brothers would sit on the floor with whichever kit it was, tools and parts in hand. Ultimately, their faces were twisted into a puzzled look, and the ever-reliable left-over piece would be lying there. No one could figure out where it belonged. This inevitably led to one of my mother's most popular phrases, "When all else fails, read the instructions." And the next decision would be, "is that piece really necessary?"

Back then, on Christmas day, it took all we had to not wake up my parents while it was still dark outside! We waited until we couldn't wait any longer. Then, we had to wait till my parents brewed their coffee and took their cups to the sitting room where we could do our stockings. The tree, with all its booty, was hidden away in the living room behind closed doors. That was saved for later, just adding to the excitement (and torture) of us kids. Because breakfast came next. Then, and only then, could we rush to the living room and dive into the awaiting surprises.

Now here we were, Christmastime 2014. We were a day away from our big Christmas Eve traditional dinner. Scott and I had done this for all the years we were together, starting in San Diego. We rented a long table for 14, I got out the good linens and china, and provided a feast for best friends whom we wanted to thank for being in our lives. What a sweet bonus of having some of my family here, too!

Macky had been told about Scott, as had Laurel and Elena. Scott called Doug and left it to him to tell his daughters. Apparently, when he did, he was concerned at first about how they'd take it. So, after telling them about "Aunt" Scott, he gingerly asked them what they thought. Without skipping a beat, they told Doug he might want to exchange the presents he'd gotten for Scott for something more feminine. Young people are just the best! The girls had no problems whatsoever, including getting pronouns correct from the start.

The time had come. I would give it a try. Scott and I had a couple of hours to ourselves for Christmas shopping. And this was the first time that she and I would be going out in public with her dressed as ... herself.

Honestly, this was one of the things I had dreaded and fought most in my head when Scott came out to me, and I would try to imagine what that would look like. And here it was. It did happen. It wasn't a product of my worry and imaginings any longer; it was real. And I was facing that scene in "Orange is the New Black" that I thought I would never, *ever* be able to face if it did become my fate. Now, face it I must. And, sure enough, I was in the bathroom with Scott saying, "Here, let me help you with your eyeliner."

Another "never" toppled.

But you know what got me? That face. I still had vestiges of my feelings of being victimized by all this, but then I saw her face—really saw her face. I saw the vulnerability and soft fear behind the eyes. And there was excitement there, too. This was something she had always wanted—to be able to look and act as the person she always knew herself to be, but was afraid to be. And I was her partner, her best friend. We had always been there for each other. This was still My Love, my mate, the one I had loved for over 25 years.

I was also beginning to develop more of a "what the Hell" muscle—meaning I was becoming more open to what life had in store for me. No, this was not predictable by any stretch of my imagination. This was certainly not how I had pictured my life and my marriage evolving, but how often do we have the life we think we're going to have? We can't predict what surprise or shock or change is going to insert itself into the course of our lives. We don't have that blueprint. We only have Jesse James—the ability to choose how we ride out what comes.

In time, I would be checking off my list of "nevers"—of things I never thought I would say to my *husband*. Right along with, "Do you want to go to Sephora?" "No, let's not look for bras at the Maidenform outlet, we should go to Victoria's Secret." Well, Victoria might have a secret, but we didn't anymore!

Scott actually did need a bra. She had been growing in that area. It's not uncommon for this to happen to a man at Scott's age, but this was different—mostly for her emotionally. She wanted to wear bras in addition to needing one. I usually didn't bother with bras myself. My hippie days were still alive and well on that subject. I thought they were uncomfortable and confining, and it's not like I had a real need. But Scott did, and I was watching this woman emerge with her own taste and style.

At the same time, there was this thought that was starting to grow in my psyche that this was to be an adventure for me—a whole new life to live, a whole different incarnation than the one I thought I'd been handed. In effect, I felt I was starting to live a wholly different life inside the span of the life I started with.

We become so many different selves in life anyway, don't we? The child with parents and whatever love, or lack of it, that sets us on our journey. Then we are the young human who has to learn … everything, and "why" is always on the tip of the tongue. As children, we are learning what this is and what that means. We are soaking up data to be applied later. When we enter our teens, we are entirely different beings. Just ask any parent! And as adulthood approaches, so do a whole new set of rules and plans and goals and likes and dislikes and friends. We have work that, hopefully, we are suited to because our interests or some motivation led us there. And, chances are, we find someone we want to be with. We may experiment with several until we feel we get it right, but, at some point, most of us will find a partner to commit to creating yet another life with—now we are a couple.

We are many people in one lifetime.

Now I was in a new lifetime of my own. Same partner; different form. Or, to borrow a phrase I first learned from Scott, "Same cake, different frosting."

I wanted the same cake, even if the frosting was different. And so, when the make-up was on and the wardrobe selected, we set out for a day of Christmas shopping.

We went to a restaurant we usually went to at Christmastime. I was so self-conscious. Would we be stared at? Would people know, give us looks? But we walked in, were shown to a table and the waiter came over to say, "What can I get you ladies?" "Ladies?" Not a flinch, not a double-take, no question in the waiter's eyes except about what our menu choices would be. No heads turned anywhere around us. Wow. Yes, it was as easy as that. I don't know how strong I would have been if someone had given us a second glance, but we passed the first test. Yet another shift happened for me. Going out with Scott … out, was something I had dreaded. I was so relieved it went the way it did, and now I saw that I might just be able to do this, accept this, and we had a wonderful, chatty, delicious lunch together. We talked like we always had, especially at this time of year—with the joy and glow of Christmas plans and family visits, and the anticipation of our Christmas Eve dinner.

I had to admit, Scott looked very attractive. This was not a man in a dress. She'd been transformed. She was at home in her skin. I was starting to think she looked better as a woman than she ever had as a man. Her walk and many of her mannerisms were now feminine. Graceful.

Ha! Maybe I was getting "in touch with my inner lesbian!" Well, no. That line still bugged me. Maybe less now, though.

And it was in this moment that it also occurred to me that people might look at us and think we're lesbians.

Not that there's anything *wrong* with that! (Thank you, Jerry Seinfeld.) But I had a hard time with that. I had been so focused on Scott and all that was swirling around us with her situation that I didn't think I would be stamped and judged by a name, a label, a group, a sexual preference that I didn't belong in, didn't relate to. Was this to be my own sampling of profiling? Even the flash of these thoughts made me uncomfortable. People could form opinions and conclusions about me just by my association with Scott.

This is when I thought there should be yet another initial added to the LGBTQIA letters: D. Yes D for "default." After all, I was only entering this world of transgender, of LGBTQ, through no fault or choice of my own. I Was Taft-Hartley'd, Red Rover'd in. I didn't identify with any of the other initials. I wasn't one of "them," I was along for the ride, so that made me part of the community by default. As I said, people would tag me as an "L," but they would be wrong. I am a cisgender heterosexual female which means I identify with the same gender I was assigned at birth and I am attracted to men. Oh, the new words I had to learn! It was like moving to a foreign country and getting the Rosetta Stone course in the language.

It's not that I think it's *bad* to be a lesbian. As you know (and you know the line), some of my best friends are lesbians. But it's the principle of the thing—of being typed and labeled as something I'm not. Now I had a whole new world to investigate inside myself, to reconcile and make peace with.

This reminds me of a funny exchange I had with a lesbian friend when I was telling her about Scott over the phone: We talked about our childhood crushes. I told her I was madly in love with Richard Chamberlain, the star of the TV show, "Dr. Kildare." Over the years, people kept insisting to me that he was gay, but I just refused to believe it. No! Not possible! He was mine! My friend, who is a lesbian, admitted that she was madly in love with Haley Mills when she was a kid. She talked about how she had to hide that for fear she'd be discovered. I admitted that I finally accepted the fact that Richard Chamberlain was gay and I would never have him. And she said, "No, but you got Haley Mills!" We laughed and laughed, and I felt a warm sense of companionship and mutual understanding.

I was starting to see that each one of us has a story. How many of us have had to hide something—hide something about our childhood we were afraid would get us in trouble? How frightening it is to feel we might be different. It makes us a potential outcast, looking at everything through a thin veil that separates us from what we thought was normal. The need to belong, to be part of something, must be one of the strongest human drives. And it's real. People are all too ready to point fingers and declare that someone else belongs outside their artificial circle.

Labeling, othering is what gets us in trouble. I've been trying to avoid labels as much as possible—using them and being defined by them. And to be falsely stamped simply by my appearance or the company I keep? Why does it matter to people? Why do we have to judge? We should all have a taste of what it does to people to misjudge them.

Words have such power! People talk about Hillary Clinton as a "career politician" as if that's a bad thing. Yet, if you use the phrase, "public servant," it sounds positive, right? I don't believe that "sticks and stones would break my bones but names would never hurt me." Sometimes names are used with the specific intent and power to inflict pain. Verbal abuse is still abuse.

OK, enough politics for now. Back to our shopping day—new discoveries all over the place. We went to Macy's in the same mall as the restaurant. As we walked through the door, the words had already formed in my mouth, "I'll meet you back here at...." But wait! I didn't need to say those words. I giggled out loud as I realized we'd be going to the same departments! We could browse together. We both wanted pajamas and leggings and lip gloss. What a trip! I could feel more of the ice of my fears melting as I realized there were some kinda fun things about this. And the glee on Scott's face only enhanced the revelation. This was a dream come true for her. A dream of decades.

We scored with the jammies ... even got ones that closely matched. Not on purpose, mind you. We just both liked the style and fabric. We each got some leggings and I looked at lip gloss.

I love the look of lip gloss. I'm forever on the hunt for something I like that will be shiny and stay on. *Never* have luck with that! And then, there's Scott. Life can be so cruel. She can put on lipstick in the morning and never have to do a touch-up all day! I put it on and it's gone practically by the time I put it away. No, I don't lick my lips that much or eat or drink ... it just ... disappears!

Okay, we're in the middle of the holidays, and have some serious celebrating and coming out to do!

Shopping was done. The time was here.

Christmas Eve was upon us. Scottie had been cooking sauces for days and was a shopping maniac. Christmas Eve dinner for 14 again. Rented tables and chairs and linens arrived, the house went through a cleaning, and the living room was rearranged so we could set up a long banquet table that would seat everyone.

And yes, you heard right, "Scottie." It was time for her name to fit her gender.

I lobbied with her for "Scottie" early on. It was a natural, it was feminine and strong, it wouldn't be a stretch for anyone. Family and friends could make the tweak without much effort. She did float out some other name choices to discuss with me, but I told her I just would never be able to call her "Stephanie" or "Scarlett" (a real consideration for a day). Besides, I liked a TV show that had a female Scottie in it, so it wasn't unheard of. Perfect! Scottie it is, and we told everyone at our Christmas Eve dinner.

The menu didn't vary much from previous years—that was a tradition. You know, there was Timpano as the main dish. If you ever saw the movie "The Big Night" (and if you haven't, do!), the Timpano was inspired by that movie. Now, because we have vegetarians in the crowd, many of the ingredients used in the movie were not possible in our version. Scottie improvised, reinvented and concocted an amazing masterpiece. She would line a large ceramic bowl with homemade dough. The recipe was her own, created by combining a couple of her favorites. Inside this timpani drum-shaped pastry were layers of different pastas and cheeses and sauces that were then topped off with a final layer of the pie dough. This was baked to golden perfection until it was time to serve by inverting it onto a large, round platter, revealing this amazing drum of yum! Oh, but that was only part of the feast, though it was the piece de resistance! There were roasted vegetables grouped on trays according to the different marinades they had bathed in for hours. There were homemade chicken meatballs rolled in truffle powder, chicken sausages and peppers, and Caesar salad.

Scottie dressed in a mini kilt, one of her Robert the Bruce Clan's tartans. She wore dark tights and boots. Her top was a white, boat-neck sweater, and her hair and make-up were perfect.

Since my family was staying with us, they were already at the house, and a few other guests started arriving early.

Scottie was putting some finishing touches to her sauces when I heard her softly say, "My Love." When I went to see what she wanted, she said, "Please don't judge me. I broke a nail."

I knew what this meant. She had been getting manicures since her time in Alaska and this was an important luxury for her. I call it a luxury, but I think she'd call it a necessity. I was used to this by now. In fact, I kept marveling at how beautiful her hands looked now—so graceful and feminine. These hands could not have been the same hands I was so taken with when I first met Scottie and was mesmerized by the way those hands controlled the lens on a large video camera. Though, even then, one of the things that attracted me to look at "Scott's" hands was how graceful those moves were, focusing the camera.

I know she wanted everything, including herself, to be perfect on this Christmas Eve, so I said, "Go! Get your nail fixed. Is there anything I have to keep an eye on?"

The look of relief and gratitude on her face touched me deeply. I was there for her, no questions asked. This was a key moment for both of us—Scottie because I got the situation instantly and backed her up, and me because I didn't hesitate in wanting to have her back. There wasn't any, "Really? It's just a nail, no one will notice, it's not a big deal." Just "Go!"

She was back in a flash and the festivities began. Smiles

and laughter, toasts of support for Scottie and for me. People could see how beautiful she looked. I could see how beautiful she looked! Her face and body were more feminine as time was passing. We could see this was right. Was everyone else one hundred percent on board? Maybe not quite yet. They had to do some rewiring of their own, work on getting their pronouns straight at the very least. That actually may have been the toughest adjustment.

We made it! We did it! Scottie and Marcy. Scott had unzipped that outer skin and stepped out into the light, into Scottie, her true self. Now I understood that experience in the Jain Temple all those years before. And now Scottie's experience of that day was as significant for me as it was for her.

Christmas Day was more of the same—pure magic. Family all gathered in our house with a fire in the fireplace, a new electric train circling the tree (my present from Santa to remind me of my childhood) … and Scottie. Scottie relaxing into her skin. All of us relaxing in our jammies, eating, opening presents, playing games, and laughing our heads off.

It was all over way too soon. Family went back to their respective homes, Scottie went back on location to finish the project she was working on, and I was home with the dogs and my thoughts.

My mother had joked that she had four boys and one's a girl. Well, I had four husbands and one's a girl!

CHAPTER 33
AND SCENE

The last tango, the crossroads, the milestone, the turning point, the fork in the road, the last exit to Brooklyn, the key to the lock; the crucial defining moment had arrived. And it all happened in a Staples.

Scottie was out of town on her shoot. Again. I was reveling in how far we'd come—how special and freeing our short time together had been at Christmas. And I was also counting on one hand the weeks we were able to spend together over the past three years, and some of those weeks were spent with me in a hospital bed or at home recuperating from chemo. Not the best quality time.

Throughout this book, I've talked about the waves of new discoveries about Scottie being trans, and my various reactions to reveal after reveal. I've talked about the discoveries I made about myself, my concepts, my expectations, my dreams and some of the rewiring I had to do.

One undercurrent, one recurring theme that I hadn't yet shaken was the feeling that maybe I still didn't really know this person. That may sound strange after all this time, but remember, for over 20 years, I'd missed that she was trans! Hello! I had no hint, no suspicion, no clues, nothing. This led me down the path to even darker, more insecure thoughts now that I was alone and had the time to stew.

I could not push out the haunting questions of what else?

She had admitted that, when she was in Denver, she would go out to bars with trans friends, dressed in female attire. I could not get the images out of my head, and I could not get over the fact that she was drinking. We had not been drinkers from the time we were serious about each other.

These were all things I put in her "secrets" column, the "betrayal" column. If all this could happen outside of our agreements as a couple, could there be more? Could she also have stepped outside our vows?

I was relieved that she was away from the Denver scene, because she was more the way I remembered from our past—calling every night after her tasks were done, chatting about the people and the stories about the production, sharing how easily she'd been accepted in her new form, telling me how much she loves me.

But what if she had stepped out and shared intimacies with someone else? That would have been the point of no return. I had already faced so much, compromised so much, rewired my beliefs about marriage and gender roles and sex and trans and relationships and love ... and me, for that matter! I had confronted ovarian cancer and surgeries and chemo. I was maxed. I had learned the lesson not to ask what else could possibly happen—because it usually did! And it felt like asking that question invited finding out there was a "what else!"

One night, I had to get out of the house. I needed a new notebook and an excuse, so I went to Staples. Staples always provides a welcome distraction as I aimlessly walked up and down the aisles of things I didn't ever need, but still was strangely drawn to.

I was in one of those sections of the store when Scottie called with her goodnight call. There I was in the Staples office furniture section.

At her end, she was walking along a moonlit path in the winter night—a snow-covered path, brilliantly lit by the moon and stars; shadows of trees and the distant mountains.... She was completely enfolded in this bucolic setting. She could wrap her coat around her and snuggle into the warmth of the down protecting her from the nighttime chill—somewhat of a contrast to my fluorescent-lit, metal and concrete building filled with office items and equipment and furniture and a handful of evening shoppers.

I was so happy to hear Scottie's voice and I loved hearing her tales of the day. But my mind was elsewhere. I was still in the dank cave of my thoughts from before, still thinking about that nail-in-the-coffin factor of questioning her fidelity. And she felt it. She always could (and can) hear my subtext, hear my voice and know there are other voices inside me clamoring to be heard.

And so, she asked, "What's going on? I can hear it in your voice."

I said, my voice soft with trepidation, "I did have one question about your time in Denver."

I heard the silence and felt her energy tighten on the other end of the line. She took a breath and talked about how she had hoped that time was behind both of us. She said it was embarrassing and a clumsy time for her as she tried to discover and reconcile who she was, tried to get answers and find a place where she belonged—not geographically, but inside her own body and mind. She hoped we would not have to talk about that time ever again. But as she was saying all this, something broke inside her. I heard it in her voice. She could tell this was not going away unless we faced it head-on.

She said, "I'll answer the question just once more so that we could be done with that chapter."

She was anticipating the question. She thought she knew what it was, or at least which one it might be out of a couple options pertaining to her going out in Denver. What she did *not* anticipate was what I asked.

In spite of where I was, I was not going to put off this question one more minute—not going to wait till I got home, not going to wait for tomorrow or for her to be done with her production, but now. So I sat down. I sat in an executive swivel chair covered in plastic in the office furniture section at Staples. I didn't care who walked by; I didn't care that the setting was so ridiculous.

I was shaking. I was so afraid of the answer. Somehow I knew she would be completely honest with me this time; she knew this was critical, whatever it was. And I stammered and shook and somehow managed to get the question out, "Did you have sex with anyone else?"

I was blown away at the energy and voice that came back to me over the phone. She sounded relieved!

She was also in disbelief. "Is *that* really it? Is that really your question? Oh my God! That one's easy! No! Never! I would never break our vows, never have sex with anyone else. And it's not just because we'd taken the oath, it's also because I never wanted to. I am attracted to you and you alone, have loved you and you alone. There could never be another, even for a meaningless fling." She continued, "If anything, with all her travels, going out in Denver, all my experiences of others back then only strengthened my love for you, my attraction to you, my fidelity to you!"

She was practically giddy with relief. It was freeing to be able to answer a question so honestly and wholeheartedly. I think it was also freeing to her that my question didn't have anything to do with her being trans. This was non-trans related. This was us. This was ours alone. Our world, our love, our intimacy, and it was safe.

How do I describe the sensation of what happened inside me in that moment? It was volcanic; it was the green flash; it was like carwash brushes were scrubbing away the film that had formed around me and cast a shadow on my heart. I was breathing again. I was relaxing into the truth of her answer, the reassurance that our bond was not broken.

And I was then amused as I took a moment to stand outside the whole scene and see how very funny it was! Really? One of our heaviest, most intimate discussions was taking place in Staples and on a deserted path in Canada? How could we help but laugh? And we did. We laughed with the accumulated years of love and closeness we had shared. We laughed with a strengthened sense of connection and renewed commitment. We laughed knowing we had tackled so much together in our lives that we were strong enough to tackle what lay ahead. Yes, to pinch a campaign slogan, we were "stronger together."

I was smiling. I was light. I was happy. I was relieved. I was in love. I was ready to face what was to come.

And there was still more that lay ahead over the next year, but the difference was we now did everything together; discussed everything together. No hiding, pretending, holding back, leaving out details. Honesty—no longer a lonely word! Still to come was Scottie's official name change and a few more steps in her transition.

One of those steps came in January 2015. Hormones. This was a topic I had dreaded and we'd argued about for a few years up to this point. From menopause on, I never wanted to take hormones. Still living my health-nut, no-drugs rule: "I don't want any horse piss in my body!"

Well, Scottie did. I got all the explanations presented with all the research and could see a former "never" was now inevitable. I could see the "whys" eventually. It was different for Scottie. She had to fight all the testosterone that had been driving her for decades prior. To be a woman, she really did need the estrogen. And it did make a difference, almost instantly. She talked about feeling her entire system was being rewired, right down to the way she thought. That was incredible! But there are lots of theories that tell us how differently men and women think. Her looks started changing more dramatically, too. Her breasts were growing and changing shape. Really? I still sometimes think to myself that it's a cruel world when your "husband" has better boobs and has lipstick that stays on all day!

Her face was also slimming and becoming sculpted into even more feminine features than what were already visible. Her figure changed too into more of an hourglass. She was getting hips and a waist. This is powerful stuff! Should I reconsider?

Besides having a name that now matched her identity, Scottie needed the new name because another next step included going to court for the official name and gender change, which meant she could get a new license, birth certificate and passport. Then there are bank accounts and creditors and the Costco card, of course.

In March, I went to court with her. She was dressed tastefully in casual business attire and her hair was pulled up from the sides with the rest down in the back. I can still remember the click, click, click of her high-heeled, peep-toe pumps on that tile floor and echoing off the walls of the corridors. It sounded deafening to me!

Soon we were in the courtroom, and the bailiff called

"Scott's" name (after getting a couple files mixed up first. A bit of a heart stopper), and Scottie walked up to stand before the judge who said, "You've petitioned for a name and gender change?"

Scottie said, "Yes, Your Honor."

And the judge said, "Granted."

Just like that! A file on a whole identity closed with a single word. We went to the clerks' office to get the paperwork, with several copies, and that was it!

I was now married to Scottie Madden, female.

You may laugh, but one thing that hadn't even occurred to me was that we now were in a "same-sex" marriage! When I realized this, it hit me like a ton of bricks! I got freaked out! After all this, could we actually no longer be legally married?!

What if the law hadn't just passed approving same-sex marriages? Luckily, it had, but ... I later learned that, because we were already married, that would not change now. But that scare did give me pause. A dear friend of the family often said in answer to that phrase, "On you they look good."

And scene.

CHAPTER 34
HOW DID I DO IT?

People continually ask me how *I* did this. What did I do to get through this winding saga and end up content with the results? I've covered much of that already. What I'll do in this chapter is recap some and add some points that weren't covered. So here goes:

It mostly boils down to examining and prioritizing. I had to constantly examine my own feelings, concepts, prejudices and even goals. Are they true? Are they based on Fairy Tales? Are they deal-breakers, or can a new perspective suggest a different outcome? Prioritizing then comes from choosing what is most important of all to me, putting that on the top of my list for what I must have, and working my way down from there.

One of the biggest supports in my journey was my circle of friends. What started out to be one of my biggest fears was how they would respond to my situation, but many of them turned out to be key influencers in my shift.

My very first attempt to talk to a friend was that day on the walk with Leslie. When I squeaked out the words that Scott thought he was a woman, Leslie took it so in stride. I felt my first wave of relief. I still remember her words to me, "Love is love."

If I had been determined to have a *husband*, a *man* in my life—If I were immovable that I was not a lesbian, and therefore could not love Scottie—that would have been one of those "deal-breakers." But Leslie chipped into my concept with just those three words.

Then there was my dear friend, Melissa, who came to visit in 2014. I wanted to tell her in person. We were close, and the idea of holding in that big secret was more than I could bear. Besides, I thought she might be understanding since one of her favorite sayings is, "I found the man of my dreams. The only problem is he has a boyfriend."

So, I fumbled the words and tried to tiptoe in.

I said, "I have something to tell you."

She said, "Oh no, what?!"

And I said, "Scott is a woman."

And her reply, as I ducked in anticipation of her shock and questions was, "Oh, thank God! I thought you were going to say you're splitting up!"

Huh? If Melissa could change gears about Scottie, could I?

And ah! There was that night in April 2015 of the full moon eclipse. My friend, Eloise, had come from San Diego to spend the night. We ended up lying on our backs out in the street to watch the eclipse. (Our street is a dead end with very little traffic).

We talked and shared and laughed, but I just couldn't bring myself to tell her that night.

That's where it gets funny because, when I did finally tell her a couple weeks later, what upset her was that I had told anyone before her! That was the issue, not Scottie being trans. She thought that, because we had declared that we were EFFs (Eternal Fucking Friends), she should have been the first to know.

I was learning big lessons about not assuming what is important to others. With each new encounter and sharing, I felt lighter and lighter. My friends were easy and light, taking it pretty much in stride.

My family was also pretty great. Some needed to learn about what trans is and what pronouns to use, but they were willing to hang with the information and make the effort to adjust to us as a new couple.

All these friends and family helped me heal the divide between my head and my heart. I had avoided talking to people at first, but talking did help. I should have trusted more and been less concerned about being judged.

From the start of this journey, my concepts and beliefs were tested and challenged. Some were falling away or under house arrest. Still others were in need of being reconciled. The process was not at all easy. Surely you know by now that I was not always calm, and loving, and accepting and supportive. I had my moments!

And I had my questions. Did she have to do this? Did she have to do this now? When did she know? Why didn't she tell me? How could she marry me knowing this, and not let me know so I could choose whether I still wanted to get married?

I cried; oh, how I cried. I screamed at the Universe, too. "Really? This, too?! You didn't think ovarian cancer was enough for me to deal with?"

After spitting that one out to the Universe, I heard a voice inside remind me of the aphorism, "God will never give you more than you can handle." Well, if God only gives you what you can handle, God has a lot of faith in me!

That one cut through to my core. That was the key. It made me feel strong. We need to deal with whatever life dishes out. I needed to live my life sitting up in the saddle, like Jesse James.

Ultimately, Scottie herself was the most important supporter of all in my side of the journey. She stayed with me through getting cancer and all that followed. She was there for me. And she made sacrifices for me. After all, much of the reason she chose to continue to pretend to be a man for all those years we were married was so that I wouldn't be hurt! How big a sacrifice was that?!

Didn't she finally deserve the right to feel happy? Whole? True to herself? Wasn't it time to stop pretending—putting her own life on hold?

These were the realizations that would creep into my consciousness over the years since she came out to me and shed light on new understandings. Over time, my position on many things was softening. What is marriage? What is a mate, a husband? What are the things most important to keep versus the others to let go?

Lots of soul searching.

Of course, during all of this, life also dealt us many distractions. Both of us were out of work and having difficulty finding anything. It caused great tension in me. I hate feeling like I don't know where the next paycheck is coming from, let alone having to rely on the generosity of friends and family to help us get through.

So, when Scottie would ask me how her outfit or her make-up was, I'd often answer, "Yeah, yeah. Your lipstick looks great, now get a job!"

And that reveals another tool that I relied on heavily—humor, humor, humor. Thank God we both have a sense of humor. Joking about things like this can lighten the load.

Everything passes. What was important one day can be forgotten the next. "Squirrel!" The movie, *Up* anyone?

My belief in karma also helped me once I reminded myself that I could not be in this situation unless I was meant to be. There are no accidents. I had a role to act out in this play and I was cast for this part. I could not hold on to blaming Scottie or God or anyone else.

The big question, the examining and prioritizing question was: ultimately, what did I want? Answer: joy in my life, love, partnership, a best friend, a lover. Had any of these things gone away? No. Scottie was all those things to me for many years. This was the person I said "I love you" to throughout every one of those years.

Though Scottie was going through a transition, I kept seeing all the things that would never change no matter what her gender identity. Who we are in our hearts, at our core, is our truest identity.

One caution before we close the book. This is a process—a process that continues and will continue. I know we will have more bridges to cross and situations to resolve. It ain't over till it's over.

At any juncture where I thought we were done, that we had passed all the hurdles, I discovered I was wrong. We made it through Scottie's first declaration that early dark morning over "fawkey" in 2008. We made it past make-up and dressing like a woman. We made it through changing her name and gender for real. We resolved the hormone issue. But we weren't done.

Though neither of us thought Scottie would ever have Gender Confirmation Surgery, she did. What had once been a never is now a reality. And we made it through—I was at her side through it all, happily. We actually had many fun moments, believe it or not!

And one more note about our amazing friends and family: When she was recovering from the surgery, Scottie's hospital room looked like a florist shop! After one of the nurses had made many trips down the hall with delivery after delivery of beautiful bouquets and gifts, she walked in the door with yet another gorgeous arrangement and said, "Really?" We were happy to adorn the front desk of the nurses' station on the day we left.

And we're not done. We can't be because this is life, and life itself is a process. We're here to have experiences that urge us to learn and grow. We can go strapped across the saddle or sitting up in it, but we're going riding, Jesse James!

Remember the Chicago song I sent to Scottie, "We Can Last Forever?" From the first time I heard it, I played it over and over and came to love it. I sent it to Scottie to let her know I wasn't giving up, but I realized that song was just as much for me! I needed to hear its message. I needed to believe we could last forever. I needed to accept we could face any challenge together.

We were still "us." We were still "we" and, if we always came back to love, we *could* last forever.

The End

ABOUT THE AUTHOR

Marcy is someone who has always followed her heart, and that includes career choices. Yes, "choices" plural—from producer to animal counselor to advocate and public speaker on behalf of transgender rights to, well, author. She volunteered for 5 years as a wildlife rehabber in San Diego, but injured and orphaned wildlife got the memo and still find their way to her door in LA. Marcy and Scottie love their Girard "treehouse" on the edge of the Santa Monica Mountain Conservancy preserve, and are ridiculously in love with their two perfect (of course) dogs, Aria and Bella.

57785921R00124

Made in the USA
San Bernardino, CA
22 November 2017